Evolution
of
LOVE
and
HATE

Paul Ross

ISBN 978-1-0980-8284-0 (paperback)
ISBN 978-1-0980-8285-7 (digital)

Copyright © 2021 by Paul Ross

All rights reserved. No part of this publication may be reproduced, distributed, or transmitted in any form or by any means, including photocopying, recording, or other electronic or mechanical methods without the prior written permission of the publisher. For permission requests, solicit the publisher via the address below.

Christian Faith Publishing, Inc.
832 Park Avenue
Meadville, PA 16335
www.christianfaithpublishing.com

Printed in the United States of America

The well-known civil rights martyr Martin Luther King Jr. wrote, "I have a dream that my four little children would one day live in a nation where they will not be judged by the color of their skin, but by the content of their character." This reference to character is actually addressing the heart of man. American Heart Association (AHA) centers for disease control and prevention and National Heart, Lung, and Blood Institute (NHLBI) all conclude that some of the ways you can maintain a healthy heart and minimize or eliminate heart disease are by not smoking, eating diets rich in omega 3 fatty acids more than once a week, laughing much and exercising regularly.

All of these recommendations require an active participation role in order for one to see and experience the full benefits. Reading about it, talking about it, watching a program, or attending a seminar on it simply provides information. This information, however, must transition from just being a hearing process to an active and continued process. Good desires, intentions, and thoughts will not allow the heart to see the full and healthy effects required without the actions needed to yield the maximum result, a healthy heart. The emphasis on having a healthy heart appears to be more and more of a central discussion in any doctors visit as society becomes more and more cognitive of the fact that our heart, the core and central organ of our existence, must be maintained in order for us to live a more vibrant and healthy life.

Interestingly there is an emotional and spiritual equivalency to a healthy heart that is often overlooked or ignored. Why is it that we often express our feelings with the use of the *heart*? We use and hear expressions such as "I love you with all my heart," or "That news broke my heart," or the other popular one, "My heart sank when I heard that news." This association with the heart is not an abstract or cultural expression that was birthed from traditions and customs, instead it is the relevant and truthful expressions, a spiritual and physical marriage of our emotions, used to describe our lives. The unfortunate aspect of this emotional and spiritual side of our heart is that it is not focused on as much as we do with the physical maintenance and its attributes.

One Bible verse from the book of Psalms chapter 119 which says, "Your word have I hid in my heart that I may not sin against you," shows the importance of spiritual maintenance to one's heart and its positive consequence.

The heart will yield whatever is planted within it. If that is negative and evil, then it will yield negativity and evil; but if love, peace, and compassion is planted, then it will yield love, peace, and compassion. As we observe the world around us, it becomes clearer that the world is in need of a spiritual and emotional cleansing. The type of cleansing and maintenance that can bring about the types of heart changes that can and will bring changes strong enough to change lives.

This desire of mine to see those around me live and walk with a healthier spiritual heart was instrumental in me writing this book. There is a process through which one's heart passes from a place of love to eventually succumb to hate if the right maintenance is not in place.

> Love must be sincere, hate what is evil; cling to what is good (Romans 12: 9)
>
> No one is born hating another because of the color of his skin, or his background, or his religion. People must learn to hate, and if they can learn to hate, they can be taught to love, for love comes more naturally to the human heart than its opposite. (Nelson Mandela)

EVOLUTION OF LOVE AND HATE

One of the powers of persuasion is the ability to guide someone else's thoughts in favor of or against a given idea or perspective. The younger my kids were, the more impressionable they were, and my wife and I learned early that we had to be careful with what we said to them—whether a promise to purchase that coveted toy they wanted or telling them that if they watched a certain television show, it would give them nightmares. Persuaded, they believed and obeyed us so as not to experience any nightmares. The promise to purchase that coveted toy was locked and loaded in their mind's chamber, and it didn't matter if it was midnight. They would still remind you that you made a promise and that they were going to hold you to it.

These early years of persuasion opened my perspective and brought the question that many do not even think of asking; how many adults are living their lives as a result of profound and successful persuasion from a television advertisement to a newspaper advertisement promoting a get-rich job anyone can start? We have all been persuaded, in some ways or another, without even thinking about it, and ordinarily these types of persuasion are similar to those I've already mentioned. The true task of determining our life's journey of persuasion comes down to our core belief on many topics. We have been conditioned and persuaded on matters of religion, politics, race, money, education, and social actions, all framing an intricate mental network on which we live our lives. This power of persuasion is so powerful that it even overrides our personal emotions and feelings about a matter. In many instances, facts are not important. The decision is automatically being processed based on a subjective and persuasive experience one has had. This is clearly seen for persons with a phobia. You and I may think of their fear as baseless. But to them, it's as real as life itself.

Just picture in your mind for a second: it's a rainy night, and you are working at the local 7-Eleven store. It's after midnight, and you moved around the store, rearranging and straightening products in their right place on the display shelves. Because of the time, the customers coming in are fewer. You are making your way back to the register when the door swings open and a young man of native American Indian ethnicity and probably eighteen years old burst through the door. Do you get nervous, curious, wonder what he is up to? Or do you simply see this individual as another customer hurrying to get out of the falling rain? Imagine this same occurrence with the individual being Caucasian or of Asian, or African, or Hispanic ethnicity.

Some individuals may have a totally different approach to this situation depending on who this person is. It is worth noting that, as humans, many of our judgment about an issue ends up being wrong.

To quote French philosopher Michel de Montaigne, "There were many terrible things in my life and most of them never happened," is to come face to face with the reality that most of those things we fear and worry about never happens. So given this approach to worry, anxiety, and fears, where do you see yourself? This question really requires reaching deep into our core to truly see, with unabashed reality, what are our thoughts on this and a host of other life events and activities in general.

The year was 1992, and on that sunny summer day in the city of Los Angeles, California, anger was stirring in the local community over a not-guilty verdict passed down by the local courts.

The four police officers were initially charged for beating a man to the point of him being hospitalized as a result of the injuries sustained during the encounter. The police officers were white, and the victim was black. Slowly the anger in the community transferred into unrest as many in the community marched into the streets chanting "no justice, no peace." This chant blossomed into a full riot as stores began to be looted and destroyed, and motorist and pedestrians were blatantly attacked without provocation. The predominant blacks and Hispanics rioting in the streets operated with an anger that had appeared to erupt like a volcano. Everything and everyone in their path automatically became a targeted enemy to be consumed by its fury. As this chaos unfolded in the community, law enforcement and medical responders were all halted from entering the zone now seen as too hostile and dangerous. Innocent individuals going about their daily business suddenly found themselves in the line of fire. Store owners watched in horror as their stores were looted, vandalized, and destroyed.

EVOLUTION OF LOVE AND HATE

On that day, thirty-six-year-old Reginald Denny was driving his truck and trying to get to his destination for delivery when with one wrong turn, found himself in the middle of the riot zone. Realizing that he was surrounded by chaos, he slowed his truck and came to a stop. Within seconds, someone was at his truck's door and had it open. Rocks and other objects were being thrown at him; and before he knew what was happening, he was being dragged from his truck and onto the road where the assault continued. Dazed, bloodied, and confused, he attempted to shield his head; but to no avail, the rocks still made its impact on his head. An iron pipe cracks his skull while kicks and punches were felt. He felt his way around, barely able to see amidst the blood flowing down across his face. He tried getting up but was kicked down again and again until he collapsed exhausted, injured, and fighting for his life. Lying in his own pool of blood, he could only think of what was going to happen next. *Will I survive or is this how it is going to end?* he thought. He made another attempt to get up and fumbled, cracked skull and all, to get back into the truck. Moments later, three good Samaritans showed up to assist him. One jumped into the driver's seat of his truck, and the others cradled Reginald as best as they could while getting him into the truck. The driver made his way, carefully weaving through the chaos in the street, first to get Reginald to the hospital. Reginald survived after intense treatment, therapy, and the fortunate rescue by those three strangers who came to his aid. Reginald was white, and both his attackers and his rescuers were black, a clash of good and evil, choice and decisions, all playing a critical role in his life on that unforgettable and terrifying day. As sad and unfortunate as it is, these types of activities and events are occurring constantly around us. In homes, schools, marketplaces, and every area of our lives are the constant display of anger, emotions, and vengeance being unleashed.

Reginald had no involvement in this chaos and riot except for making the wrong turn onto that street on that given day. His guilt or terror was simply induced because he was white and in that given location, a non-white zone where anger and emotions and stereotypes and all came boiling and bubbling to the surface of many of the minorities in that community. Vengeance was simply being unleashed, and it was void of bias or apprehension. It is the world we live in; one that we would love to see through a different lens, but the reality comes at us with sincerity and ferocity to grab our attention. The hope in that moment is that you are on the side of mercy and grace.

After all, our sole inner goal has always been to survive the attack and assault regardless of the assault types. The intensity of exploring our world's whirlpool of hate, love, bigotry, and biases can be humbling, sad, revealing, or convicting. This assessment can yield different reactions, but ultimately my hope is that it creates an assessment result that pushes us to be better persons and leads us to embrace an unyielding faith in Jesus Christ.

> Above all, keep fervent in your love for one another, because love covers a multitude of sins. (1 Peter 4:8)
>
> Love me or hate me, both are in my favor. If you love me, I will always be in your heart. If you hate me, I will always be in your mind. (William Shakespeare)

Chapter 1

What would cause an individual to hate another, to ignore someone in help, to hurt someone deliberately, or to spread malicious information, possible lies about another? Even further, what would cause someone to hate another simply because he or she were white, black, Latin, Asian, Indian or any other nationality, race, or ethnicity different from theirs? From an early age, I have pondered those questions and have found the reality very disheartening. At the same time, the fact that no one is born a racist or a bigot, the same as no one is born a singer or a gymnast, offered hope to what seems like an unbalance or unfair world. For me, true faith in God and the acceptance that he is real and that he lives in me brings a transformation that no other person, thing, or environment could bring. True change is a process that resonates from the core of an individual and rises to the surface to reveal the true person, their character. My belief in God is just that, my belief. And therefore as you read this, if your belief is one void of any recognition of God, then that is your choice and conviction. I know the personal inward reward I have received by embracing God. I want to challenge you to look beyond your familiar circle as you open your mind to discover the truth.

Our lives exist and are managed by many conditions and emotions. Some of these conditions and emotions are regulated by natural inherent biases—for example, a parent wants to see his or her child attending the best schools, getting the best jobs, and enjoying the best things in life.

That desire is one that places their child first in line over others. This is natural and only becomes abnormal when that inherent bias is shifted to allow for the mistreatment or negative actions toward another child so that your child gets ahead. The normal and rational approach should be "I would rather my child achieve the child of the year, or receive that prestigious award on the job," but the bias should stop short of you wanting the other child to get hurt, failing their classes, losing their jobs, or other such negative actions. When we see these day-to-day inherent biases being overrun with the abnormalities, we should be concern because there is an underlying factor that is contributing to this behavior.

What we are taught and what we learn from our parents, from our siblings, from our peers all channel us to be who we are, and it is on this premise that I have decided to explore the topic of this book, the evolution of love and hate.

Many of us have grown up hearing things said by our peers, parents, siblings, teachers, even our priest, and religious leaders that have left a permanent impression on our minds. We all can identify with one or more of these things; and even as you read this, one of those fixed impressions or stereotypes comes to your mind. Many of us have heard or even utter things that were disparaging, negative, or hateful about others. At times, these comments may be directed at an ethnicity, race, work class, or other areas in life. Some individuals learned these expressions or jokes and terminology from others, and they really never understood the true meaning behind the words. It is important to know that their ignorance of the magnitude or meaning of what they are saying does not remove the impact of the words. There is a free fall of integrity, humanity, and basic morality that occurs when we allow negative, vile, and degenerative thinking to blossom. This type of thinking only creates a monster, and the results leave those of us observing this state in bewilderment. Often we would ask what would cause someone to commit a heinous act when we hear of atrocities and crime. Answering them really requires taking a serious look at the origins and source for the hate, the bitterness, and the degeneration.

Born and raised in Guyana, South America, and now a naturalized US citizen of African descent, I sometimes cringe when I hear people make the statement to me, "You are a different black guy," or the other common statement, "You are not like other black guys." What does this mean? I am usually left pondering the true meaning of those expressions toward me. Many think nothing of it to make a statement like that without even realizing that some explanation may be warranted.

I have become more and more adjusted to these subtle or naive forms of bigotry and stereotypes. Or even further, innocent ignorance is what I call it. The truth is, like any other groups of people, the black group of people has law-abiding citizens, not-so-law-abiding citizens, the poor, the middle class, and the wealthy. It becomes apparently clear to me when I hear statements like the ones mentioned above directed to me that the individual may either be delusional, naive, ignorant, emotionally traumatized, or simply innocently misled. Whenever these experiences occur, I hope the latter is the truth of the matter. I look in awe sometimes as I realize that here stands an individual who thought they were educated or informed or even versed on the issue of race relations but are really either completely ignorant of life outside their box, misinformed, emotionally scarred, traumatized, or maybe the ugly truth of being a bigot.

It is very true that we are products of our environment. These environments are your family, your neighborhood, your schools, your employment, even your church group, and the people you associate with the most. I remembered moving to Green River Wyoming in 2006 with my wife and, at that time, our only child who was less than a year old. With approximately eighteen thousand for the population at that time, the people lived lives that were typical of small-city folk.

You kept your business to yourself unless you didn't mind the whole community knowing of it.

Of course, one of the first things we noticed after moving there was the small number of minorities, particularly individuals of African heritage. We saw some, but these sighting were few and far in between.

One day, I went to the local movie rental with my son to rent a movie for the evening. Holding my son in my arm, I browsed through the aisles, reviewing the available movies. As I came around one corner, I came face to face with a Caucasian family, which were a man, a woman, one boy about seven years old, and a girl about five years old, all walking and browsing through the movies in that row. As the five-year-old girl looked up at me and my son, she screamed, "A black man!" as she turned and ran back to the adult man I would say was her father. I smiled as I held my son close and I hurried by not wanting to startle her more. I observed the older child putting his hand over the little girl's mouth and whispering something to her I could not hear. Was this just a wild fluke occurrence, or was that child thought to believe that blacks—or even worse, black males—were thieves, murderers, evil individuals, and this was the imagery that she saw at my appearance. I can only imagine. If this is indeed the circumstance for that child, then unless those thoughts are shattered along the course of her childhood life, she will grow up to be an individual that is a bigot. Sad, isn't it? What a personal prison for one to live in for his or her lifetime. I mentioned a prison because that is exactly what it is. A person that is a racist is the one that is hurting the most. These persons are trapped in their mind by the recurring nightmare of assumptions, biases, experiences, misinformation and cyclone thinking.

These individuals have had a bad or many bad experiences molded into their way of thinking. Many have emotional scars and dysfunctional perspectives that have altered their ability to think rationally and operate in mainstream society in regard to other ethnic or racial groups. Others mask it well, like an undercover alcoholic, putting up a good front in the public while wasting away behind closed doors. Thank God. There is hope for these individuals.

It is true that a lot of the bigotry and racism we see in our society today are a direct result of the customs, norms, and idealism that have been passed down from generation to generation. And the truth is, there is more than just a custom or tradition or even a belief that has been passed down. There are those underlying experiences that can also leave an indelible impression on many. Who will succumb to these experiences? And who will dare shake the custom and belief to explore the truth on their own? Unfortunately many do not, many cannot because what they know and believe is as good as life and death itself.

If you look at toddlers playing together, it is clear that hatred and stereotype are not inherited attributes but more of a learned behavior and an outlook on life. Knowing this, it is sad to think that such precious little ones could be influenced to be so positively wrong. We see this type of brainwashing or solid impression setting as we study the young Jihadist radical Muslim who teach their young in schools to hate and see to the promotion of a total eradication of the non-Muslim and western civilization. As disturbing as this sounds, it is a reality for many. The number one influence of racism and bigotry is a passing down of customs, traditions, and belief from family, friends, and associates, all working together to mold a perspective and belief into the mind of an individual.

I recalled coming upon an article online written by NY Times author Susan Chira that I thought was very interesting and revealing. It read,

> In 1986, Japanese Prime Minister Yasuhiro Nakasone remarked that the average American intellectual standard is lower than the average Japanese standard because of the blacks and Hispanics in the US. He has often said that the source of Japan's strength lies in its "racial homogeneity."

Eleven years later, University of Texas law school professor Lino Graglia triggered a firestorm of criticism for his remarks:

> Blacks and Mexican Americans are not academically competitive with whites in selective institutions. It is the result primarily of cultural effects. They have a culture that seems not to encourage achievement. Failure is not looked upon with disgrace.

What a misguided insight. It is obvious that these statements were made from the bowels of someone who, though innocent and passionate in their belief, was guided by impressions, experiences, and stereotypes that had significantly influenced both gentlemen's lives. Is it possible that if they had experiences along with other positive impressions and stereotypes like I have had, their perceptions would be different? For instance, if one spends time in the beautiful region of the Antarctic with the majestic polar bears, would that person be considered naive if he or she reports that the region was chaotic with ice and cold temperatures along with water holes all over? Imagine they continued; the Polar Bears seemed passive and lethargic, often pouncing on the ice in an attempt to break through it with no apparent reason and sometimes even diving into the freezing cold water. Imagine the impression created for those who had no knowledge of the fact. Of course, those of us who know better understand that these bears generally conserve their energy which would explain what appears to be a lethargic nature. We also know that the pouncing on the ice is not random or boredom but an attempt to break through the ice to get at a tasty meal of a seal hidden beneath the ice in its cave.

In a nutshell, these magnificent creatures are surviving. I am a firm believer that for anyone to make an assessment of any situation, condition, or even more any matter of life, he or she must first be willing and ready to stretch their research outside the boundaries of their box of ideas, impressions, stereotypes, customs, and comfort. Failure to do so would simply result in information that is inconclusive and, in most cases, inaccurate. I have lost count of the many black families I know who have no interaction with whites. No whites have ever visited their homes, and they have never visited a white's home. The same is true for many whites and other ethnic groups who pretty much stay within their familiar circle. Each of these groups may live within their own social, cultural, and ethnic world.

Some who do crossover to mingle with other groups are doing so with elements of that group that simply contributes to the stereotypes. My question is this: how could each of these families or individual honestly and accurately assess the state of a group or entire race of people outside of theirs? The answer is clear. It is impossible. For to make an assessment in this circumstance is done so based on ideas, impressions, and stereotypes that are all void of the one important and necessary element. That element is the relationship experience with all of its facts.

Today my wife and I have four beautiful kids, three boys and one girl. My girl was born one year after we moved to Wyoming. Now I can write, at length, a well-informed biography of each of them to date. Why is this? Simple, I have been with them from the day they were born. They live with me and my wife in the same house. We go to the same places. We go on vacation to the same places and at the same time and know the same people. My point is this. I could not make a comprehensive statement about my neighbor's son or daughter like I could about my own. The answer is clear. The relationship I have with my son and daughter is different from the relationship I have with the neighbor's. My assessment of the neighbor's kids will only be based on the impression I have from seeing them from time to time in the yard playing. I do not see them in their home or at social event where I am attending or on vacation or in their schools. I do not see them when they are hurting or crying or sad. I do not see them when they are embarrassed and how they react to different emotional circumstance. My point is simple: when we speak of other humans, relationship makes assessment accurate. Without the relational element, our assessment remains fractional.

In Hollywood, we see this type of relational exposure as actors and actresses submerge themselves into preparing for a role. They may spend time with the people or person to be portrayed. They may visit an environment to personally garner that experience in order to portray it with conviction and reality in their work. The same holds true for our politics; head of states from different countries travel around the world to meet and spend time with other leaders with the hope that they could build a relationship and obtain a better understanding of their needs and thoughts.

As an American male of African descent who happens to hold a graduate level degree, is married to one wife, who also has a graduate degree and an MD as a trained pediatrician and lives in the same home with our four kids, is a hard worker and does not belong to a gang, has never used illegal drugs, and has never been convicted of anything past a speeding ticket, taught college-level business course as an adjunct faculty member, I find statements like the university's professor and the former Japanese prime minister I referenced earlier leaving me curious and appalled. I suppose I experienced these emotions because my initial reaction is to think that these educated men should have known better, but I was quickly reminded that academic advancement, though good, does not alter the state of one's heart, nor does it remove the implant of a lifetime of deposited experiences, inherited stereotypical thinking, perceptions, and yes, in most cases, downright ignorance.

It is true that the African American community have had to combat the self-consciousness and the subconsciousness of years of inhuman and subhuman treatment. The deep-seated trace of worthlessness still plagues many in the communities and sadly empowers those who look on with misinformed, stereotyped, and bigoted perceptions. This still does not change the fact of the matter. Strangely enough many in the African American community succumb to the stereotype as curse through which they now live. My father once told me, "Son, blacks are a special people created by the creator. And like diamond and other precious minerals, there is a constant battle by others to obtain, control, and manipulate our destiny." He taught me and my siblings to be bold, to pursue knowledge and a relationship with God for in doing so, the sky alone is our limit.

Unfortunately many do not have the mentoring and guidance I and many other blacks are privileged to have. In my world, perceptions and goals and dreams are without limit because of this upbringing. Today I am imparting the same to my children to change and impact future generations. And guess what, this message is to any race or ethnic group, not just for me or for blacks but to all.

Inherent biases are the reality of many abuses, hate, execution, or bad attitude directed at others.

It really requires self-actualization not just of yourself but of humanity that will allow you to begin to treat others the way you would want to be treated. Here is a profound advice given to us by the Bible that goes to the core of the matter. It says in Matthew chapter 7, verse 12, "So whatever you wish that others would do to you, do also to them." Would it not be hypocritical for us to expect to be treated nice, to be respected, to be loved, to be protected, and to be given those considerations that are pleasing, but we ourselves then operate differently toward others as we demonstrate meanness, lies, hate, and disrespect toward others? This is simply a result of our heart's compass. You see the heart will not pretend. It may masquerade for a time; but eventually and like a volcano slowly churning below the surface, there will be an explosion which will reveal the content of what was so well-hidden.

If you were to visit many metropolitan cities and take a visit to the local animal shelter, you will be shocked and heartbroken at the sight of so many dogs that were beaten, abused, neglected, starved, and left to die. You will find in many of these shelters rottweilers and pit bulls that were severely maimed and left for dead. Some were used in underground fighting environments and once injured, were quickly disposed of by their handlers without treatment to sometimes life-threatening injuries. Others were kept by individuals who lacked the ability to care for the animal but simply possessed them as a matter of status to instill fear in others. It should also be noted that persons having these dogs must understand their origin. You see, the rottweiler was originally used as cattle herders because of their large profile. This instinctive nature allows this breed to be protective. This protective nature gives it the reputation of being overly aggressive.

Similar to the rott, the pit bull was used primarily for hunting. This hunting may have involved large or small game. Today these animals are primarily used in households as domesticated pets or as many with these animals would say "another member of the family, just like a child."

My brother Mark had a rottweiler he called Champ. I remembered the first time I came face to face with Champ. My reaction was to stay clear, look for a blockade between it and me. It was about three feet high with a head the size of a basketball. Shiny Jet-black coat and paws the size of an adult human fist gave me some anxiety as he came bounding across the yard to greet my brother. My brother assured me there was nothing to worry about. And before I knew it, Champ was playfully pawing at my chest as he stood on his hind legs before dropping and rolling over a few times and then repeating his face-to-face greeting. Like a child, he made me relax, and I remembered thinking, *Wow, this large dog is so wimpy*, because he was nothing like the stereotype I held of an aggressive, unpredictable attack beast. That day, my brother and his rott taught me a lesson in stereotype. If you simply live by them, then it is just about fair to say you will miss out on some incredible experiences in life.

Since life itself is a makeup of our experiences, learned stereotypes, our environment, biases, and those inherent beliefs deposited in us from whenever by whomever when we can barely remember, how do one live a life that maximizes every opportunity? Many cannot. They are unable to because they are still held as a prisoner to the conditioning they received along the way. Though part of me still takes caution with pit bulls and rottweiler, it is the same caution I take when I see a dog without a leash. I am vulnerable to the attack of any dog if it feels threatened, lacks training, or is provoked. Because of that fact, I no longer walk around fearful of dogs but simply look out for those that may be renegades. These principles are the same with our human interactions. Some of my best relationships with others were started with cautious optimism and, yes, prejudices that I had to consciously rise above to discover what the real core of that person was. Once those walls of biases and suspicions were removed, it is amazing the distance genuine relationship will take you.

> You therefore have no excuse, you who pass judgment on another. For on whatever grounds you judge the other, you are condemning yourself, because you who pass judgment do the same things. (Roman 2:1)
>
> Judging someone doesn't define who they are. It defines who you are. (Author Unknown)

Chapter 2

I remembered the first time on a particular job I held. The first day when I met with my supervisor, she seemed aware and self-assured of her expectations, her goals, her passions, and, yes, even her legacy. She eyed me across the table with an intense glare that was void of familiarity. I smiled and remained composed. After all, this was my first day on the job. There is no way she could be judging me already since I just started the job. I soon found out how wrong I was for in me, she was going to right all the wrong committed under her leadership in this department before I arrived.

By my second meeting with her, it was crystal clear what her goals and plans were because I soon realized that her expectations and goals were larger than I could fulfill. With that came the awareness that I was in a no-winning situation. My predecessor implemented processes and plans for different applications that I was now tasked to update. Ordinarily this would be fine except that my initiatives were clearly defined, and it was to make the plans, the tasks, the formats bigger, better, error-free, and within my first six months on the job.

Adding to this challenge, I now was tasked to build a case against those renegade employees who may have crossed her and gotten away with it. I was going to be the "cleaner," and I found out really soon that if my approach in managing any personnel situation was not up to her standards, you guessed it, I would see and hear of it in a personal one-on-one meeting with her which always had a document created for my personnel file. I drove home many evenings, wondering if this was a nightmare I was going to suddenly awake from, but the drive into work the following day only served to remind me that it was all a reality, my unfortunate reality.

I found myself constantly creating a conflict between her and me, which was not intentional. It was happening as a result of me attempting to implement some processes and standards on my own and thinking it would yield great success that everyone would eventually notice. This thought seemed rationale, especially since I was a department head and was specifically brought on to turn things around. The problem with my enthusiastic approaches, it was not my supervisor's plans or ideas, and she saw and interpreted all of this as going against her perfect plans, her goals, and, yes, even her legacy.

It was in the middle of the Thanksgiving and Christmas holiday when I painfully walked away from that job, a year and a half after relocating from out of state with my family. I was now sitting unemployed and praying to God for direction on what to do next. After what appeared to be a perfect career, I, like many, had suddenly found myself in a vulnerable place, being unemployed. I had a decision to make, a decision that involved my emotions and how I was going to be looking at life going forward. Was I going to be bitter toward this supervisor or feed on the slew of negative thoughts that attacked my mind. Thoughts that showed me her as hateful, vengeful, lonely, confused, and more. I instead chose to see her as needing God and truly needing to experience his love. For me, pushing away the negative thoughts allowed me to see her as she was, vulnerable and lonely and attempting to satisfy her life through external measures. This is the essence of failed humanity from the beginning of time as they attempt to fulfill a life but doing so, void of God's strength and wisdom. I found a redemption in walking away from that job. It was liberating and the start to a destiny God had in store for me that included the extinguishing of the pressures and stresses of that year and a half job. The hate and anger that was directed at me from this supervisor during the time I was employed can clearly be identified with pain, agony, and experiences she had before I arrived on the scene; I only became the sacrificial one, a seemingly easy prey on which she attempted to offset her mistakes and insecurity. There was one very important thing missing from her plans for me, and it was any knowledge that God had a promise for me straight from the Bible in Jeremiah chapter 29, verse 10. "For I know the thoughts that I think toward you, says Yahweh, thoughts of peace, and not of evil, to give you hope and a future." If only she knew the defense team I had in place, she may have reconsidered her plans. But no, what really happened was God capturing her plans and transforming it into his already existing plans for me.

You may find yourself in situations as you live your life. In some instances, you may be the victim and others the perpetrator. You may feel justified in your actions or feel unfairly treated.

Regardless of where you are, I have news for you: there is a higher power that weighs the balances of justices, time, and morality itself. You no longer need to chase the agony of wrestling with secret thoughts of revenge, shame, guilt, anger, and other emotions. The revelation in this book that I received through studying the Bible and establishing a personal relationship with Jesus Christ brought about change that allowed me to stand with my head high, whether in the low moments of life or on the mountaintop moments of my life. The Bible says in John chapter 8, verse 31 that if you study the word of God that is found in the Bible, then you will know the truth, and it will set you free.

I could not write this book without including some of the experiences that I and my family have had along the way. These experiences have taught us valuable lessons in life and continues to guide our actions today. I believe experiences are like history—the statement often said about history, "If you do not learn from it, chances are you will end up repeating it." Now this is obviously referring to the negative history we know that is marred with the negative ebb of time because no one is concerned about repeating positive experiences.

On the subject of race, I mentioned experiences along our lifetime greatly influences our perceptions; and I have to admit it takes strength, intelligence, and for me personally, a firm belief in God to be able to view life's experiences objectively. I have heard so many times where individuals claim a given experience in their life caused them to become racist, and I had often considered those individuals to be weak-minded until I began to realize the strength and ability of emotion and experiences in our lives. Emotion can guide us through paths we would rather not go and afford us decisions we would later regret. What then is the control factor to an emotional decision? Faith in God is mine and has been for some time. I have to admit there were times when I allowed my ego and emotions to lead the way and guide my impressions. I began realizing the difference of these forces' effect on the individual, and that is when I began to see things change for the best in my life. It is always refreshing to me to see people reacting positively to negative experiences they may have had. These individuals chose to take the negative and turn it into something positive, something beautiful. Christian minister Chuck Swindoll wrote the well-known poem on attitude, simply titled "Attitude." He wrote,

> The longer I live, the more I realize the impact of attitude on life. Attitude, to me, is more important than facts. It is more important than the past, than education, than money, than circumstances, than failures, than successes, than what other people think or say or do. It is more important than appearance, giftedness or skill. It will make or break a company, a church, a home.
>
> The remarkable thing is we have a choice every day regarding the attitude we will embrace for that day. We cannot change our past... we cannot change the fact that people will act in a certain way. We cannot change the inevitable. The only thing we can do is play on the one string we have, and that is our attitude... I am convinced that life is 10% what happens to me and 90% how I react to it. And so, it is with you... We are in charge of our attitudes.

Two experiences which occurred in my family brought home to me some tough realities of life.

EVOLUTION OF LOVE AND HATE

Once again it was our fortitude and faith that kept us afloat during these times, with this question to ponder: was this race, or was this random? These two experiences, though not the only experiences we have had, brought emotions to the surface that were strong. How should we react? And what should we do? Who would help us?

My wife and I were traveling to visit our family living in South Carolina; and at the time, we only had one child, our first son who was fifteen months old. We were flying out to celebrate my Dad's seventieth birthday. Since we lived in Green River, Wyoming, and had to travel three hours to Salt Lake City Airport for our plane, we decided to get to Salt Lake the night before and check into a hotel which would give us some time to have a rested night without waking too early to drive three hours to the airport. We got a great start that morning of the flight. We were rested. We made it to the airport on time, and we had checked in our baggage and made it to our flight departure gate.

It was time to board. The call was made for travelers with small kids, along with those needing special assistance, to board first. We made it onto the plane with our boy and settled into our seats. We were about to experience what so many travelers have experienced before. That experience at the time was a delayed flight due to a mechanical problem. Whew! We were already sitting on the plane now for thirty minutes when this announcement came. After about forty-five minutes of waiting and sitting, our son started to get restless as he wanted to stretch his legs as most fifteen months old would do. Now for those of you who have kids, you can relate. Our boy is all boy, energetic and curious, and so this period of sitting in one place on this full airline was a bit too much for him, and he started crying. We tried to stop the crying by offering some of his toys we brought along, but this did not work. He simply just wanted to walk. At this point, my wife and I are looking at each other thinking, *God help us.* The atmosphere on this airline was tense as passengers wondered if this flight was ever going to depart. Here we were sitting in a plane, now for forty-five minutes, with no air condition or even some television. We just sat there staring, staring out the window for those close to the windows, staring around the plane's cabin, staring at the attendants who brushed by occasionally. Jr., our boy, kept fussing and wanting to walk.

Our beautiful morning now seemed to be falling apart, with the time now almost one hour without moving. As we endured all of this, a hand appeared from behind us with a folded note. My wife took it and began reading it. We were shocked at what this note read. It read, "Sir/ma'am, with the annoying child, I have kids and they would never behave like this. Is your child deaf or retarded? I think it is rude to have such an annoying child. You should consider the feelings of the rest of the passengers on this flight. Signed, Frustrated Passenger." Wow! Indeed, this took the breath right out of my wife and me.

In a frantic effort to defend our son and our position, my wife grabbed a pen and a piece of paper to respond with only one problem, we had no idea who passed the note. In frustration, my wife broke down in tears. At that time, one of the attendants came by to ask if we wanted to take the kid for a walk as she apologized for the inconvenience of the delay. While trying to control my own emotions, I turned to my wife, telling her not to let it get at her, and I accepted the offer from the flight attendant and took our son for a walk down the ramp as I fought a million possible ways I should retaliate. While I was gone, my wife's crying became worst as she thought about the insensitivity of the individual who passed the note. A flight attendant came by to ask her if she needed any further assistance, and my wife could only respond by passing the note to her.

After scanning the note, the flight attendant gasp in disbelief as she exclaimed, "Who gave this to you!" My wife responded by motioning in the direction behind our seats. "This was totally uncalled for, and we will get to the bottom of this." the attendant promised. Before I returned to the plane with Junior, the note was passed to the pilot's cabin. And after he read it, he personally came back to directly speak with my wife. He and other attendants began asking the persons sitting behind us who passed the note. One lady sitting directly behind my wife motioned in the direction of the man sitting behind her and identified him as the person who passed the note. The man was asked to accompany the attendant to the pilot's cabin. When he arrived there, he was asked why the rude and insensitive note, and he mentioned being tired after flying all day and just needed some peace. He was told he owed us an apology to which he refused to do. At this time, the pilot made a decision. I came walking back into the plane just as all of this drama unfolded and was in time to see the man as he was summoned by the flight crew to the pilot's cabin.

The decision was made to bar him from that flight effective immediately, and he was unable to fly with this particular airline for the next three months due to his insensitive and rude behavior to fellow passengers. That made us feel somewhat better, but what an experience this was. This man had inflicted an emotional blow to my wife and me by insulting our precious boy with names like deaf and retarded. I felt anger rising up within me to the point of reaching out to get my hand on this individual's neck as he walked by. I did not give into that moment of emotional frenzy, but I did have to decompress a rush of emotions. Now this experience left us shaken but not to the point of labeling every white male as an insensitive bigot. Why? Simple, my experiences and relationship with many whites taught me that this behavior was not the norm but rather the exception to the norm. Life goes on.

Just imagine me and my wife not having any relationship with whites prior to this experience and just being fed the negative stereotypes that so well permeates our society from one group to the next. Could you see how easy it would have been to see this experience as a conformation to whites being negative and racist toward persons of color? Simply put, we have to remember American sociologist and social psychologist W. I. Thomas's words referring to stereotypes, "If people believe something to be true, it will be true in its consequences." Though W. I. Thomas was primarily referring to religion in sociology, the underlying takeaway is that our beliefs are instrumental in molding our perspectives and even convictions in life. Was this individual on the plane rude, insensitive, inconsiderate, and angry, and wanting us to disappear at that moment in time? Yes, he was. It still requires us as individuals to weigh experiences through lens not mired in negativity but also through common sense, empathy, and sympathy. This raises us above the circumstance to empower us beyond understanding. Like a father of a murdered child forgiving the murderer or an abandoned child who later forgives and accept the parent who abandoned them, taking this position somehow empowers the individual and strips them of the bondage that ordinarily holds them captive in that negative thought and experience.

Personal experiences really are at the core of our development. These personal experiences may be from things we have heard or things we have seen or things we learned even in a classroom setting; they all encompass our core beliefs of operating. Anyone void of personal experiences might as well be dead. After all, it is our living and interacting with others and with our environment that internally and mentally catalogs this series of personal experiences. The longer we live, the more we are able to tap into those experiences to use as guides along the way. The significant question then is, what type of guidance is the memory recall of our personal experiences? How do they make you a better person? If my neighbor is being attacked, I will try to intervene. I would appreciate the same efforts and consideration be given to me if I were the one being attacked. I do not allow a bad experience I had along the way to prevent me from simply helping someone. After all, tomorrow the table may very well be turned. This is my reasoning. This is my logic, and it's common sense. But then again, our world seems to be slowly opening the barrel of precious common sense, sympathy, and empathy to allow it to drift or slowly drain away bit by bit. God help us if we enter into an age where common sense, sympathy, and empathy become extinct.

When we discuss the issue of bigotry, it can become a very uncomfortable conversation and one that most would rather not have. Like religion and other hot-button topics, racism and bigotry reveal deep emotional positions that are dug into the chasms of our heart. When these emotions are stirred, the results may be catastrophic. This is because many of these emotional association and identification are rooted in a solid foundation of experiences, good or bad. With every new day that we live, there is the possibility to gain a better understanding of a matter—that is, if one is mentally and emotional capable of altering their current position of that matter.

EVOLUTION OF LOVE AND HATE

I remembered many years ago as a young Air Force personnel with the civil engineering squadron, I was stationed in Colorado Springs at Peterson Air Force Base. At the time, each person from my unit had the experience of being on call after hours for a one-week period, which rotated through the crew, giving us all an equal opportunity. This one cold, snowy night, I received a call on my on-call pager requesting someone to respond to the officer's temporary quarters on the military base. I got dressed and was a bit nervous because I was heading to the big bosses' accommodations. The thought made me a little two striper very nervous.

I arrived at the apartments that looked more like a hotel, got out my little tool bag, and headed in to find the room that sent out the call. I made it to the door and nervously knocked. I held my breath to control my nervous breathing when I heard someone beginning to unlock and open the door. An elderly gentleman opened the door. I pulled myself together and asked, "Good evening, sir, how can I help you? I'm with CE (civil engineering)." He motioned for me to come in. I glanced around the room and observe the colonel insignia as he continued, "Even though the room is not bad, I just can't seem to get any airflow from these units." He waved his hand back and forth across the top of the radiant heater which ran along the base of the wall. Now if you are familiar with radiant heat, you will know there is no mechanical-assisted air movement but instead relies on the scientific factor of hot air being less dense will rise and cold air being heavier or denser will fall. This natural behavior of air allows for a natural and silent air circulation in a space referred to as the convection effect. This constant cycling of warmer air rising and colder air falling allows the temperature in the room to be regulated to a set temperature.

I smiled patiently as he explained what he thought was occurring and thought, *How do I explain this matter to him without making him feel ignorant?* I pulled myself together again and explained to him the theory of convection with the radiant heating. He looked at me for a long second and said, "Hmmm, that's interesting. I didn't know that. Thanks for stopping by." I finally could breathe and exited the room after wishing him a good night.

I have no doubt that gentleman was intelligent, but in this single incident, he was clueless and operated only on what he thought was the norm. That night, I am sure I expanded his understanding of heating and ventilation applications, or did I?

We should allow our experiences to guide us to better understand the fact of the matter. It should open our understanding to make us better than the moment, second, day, or year prior to that experience. How would your life be different ten years ago if you knew then what you know today?

I am always assessing my motives, as well as the motives of others. Since we all have them, motives that is, then the question really is about the type of motives we harbor. What good thoughts or bad thoughts are you cultivating and allowing to saturate your consciousness and unconsciousness? One of my favorite biblical passages is Philippians chapter 4, verse 8, it says, "Finally, dear brothers and sisters, one final thing. Fix your thoughts on what is true and honorable and right and pure and lovely and admirable. Think about things that are excellent and worthy of praise." In other words, why allow yourself to be consumed with that which can ultimately destroy you. This is the reality. A rapist did not become a rapist when the act was committed. The act was simply the final results of rapist's thoughts that were cultivated and meditated upon. In the end, there is destruction and demise. The interesting thing about all of this is that within each of us is the potential and capability to be as vile and evil as any such person. This same reasoning is attributed to those who are bigots or bullies or domestic abusers.

Before the action, there were the thoughts, and those thoughts were cultivated. The saying you are what you think is based on this reasoning. Again, the scriptural equivalent for me is found in Luke chapter 6, verse 45, which says, "Out of the abundance of the heart, the mouth speaks." His or her words and actions and deeds are the true makeup of who we really are.

The "stand your ground" law may appear to be a "good citizen" recipe for protection, but the reality of such laws and regulation are predicated on fears, assumptions, bias, and prejudices. Two individuals may exhibit the same behavior and actions, but one may be spared and another executed. Why? Simply put, the victim makes the determination; and within those seconds or minutes, he or she assesses a situation while accessing a database of their own. What is in your database?

Many years ago, before my parents had any kids, they were newlyweds, and young Christian pastors of a small rural village church in the eastern region of Guyana. The area they were serving in as pastors was predominantly populated by East Indians. And in fact, the majority of the members who made up their small congregation at the time were Indians. During these years in Guyana, racial tension primarily between the two largest ethnic groups, the black and Indians, was at an all-time high. Persons were being killed, kidnapped, and beaten up in the street by opposing groups simply because of their race. My parents recount looking out of their window one day as a group of men ambushed and terribly attacked a lone individual without provocation.

My parents rode a motorcycle as their primary vehicle source. Without a car, it was difficult to intervene as this individual was beaten within inches of his life before the renegade group disbanded. One evening, they were preparing to attend an evening service at the church when hours before the schedule service there was a knock at their door. When my dad opened the door, there stood a lanky Indian young man, possibly in his twenties. Nervously he pressed into the doorway and quickly warned them to stay in that night because there was a plot in the works to ambush and kill them both. Following this disclosure, he quickly slipped away. That evening, heeding the warning, they stayed in and contacted the church to let them know in summary what was happening.

I shared this because without doing anything wrong or saying anything derogative to anyone in that community, my parents still found themselves targeted because of the color of their skin.

The individuals plotting against them did not know them either but again were fueled by the construct of negative and prejudicial databases perpetuated by the constant cultivation of this hate and the distaste and the bigotry that they nurtured inside. The young man who risked his own life to warn them was Indian and, in fact, was one of the members who worshipped at the small community church congregation. In spite of this experience, my parents continued to serve that community for several more years until they accepted another assignment in a different region of the country. The interracial relationships that were developed during those times are stronger today, decades later. Why? My parents, as well as others in that churning climate of hate and anger, chose to simply love and to simply treat others the way they wanted others to treat them.

Many years ago, I asked a college executive if it would be possible to write a letter of recommendation for me. This individual was the first person who promoted me to my first supervisory position. I recalled she wrote in that recommendation letter, "I admire the way you treat others regardless of their position in the organization." I really had not thought about that until I read those words and realized she was speaking of me. This motto had been instilled in me from my parents. They followed the biblical text that said, "Love the Lord your God with all your heart and your neighbors as yourself." Unfortunately, much of society's perspective is the opposite: you love me. I may love you. You hate me. I will hate you. Because of this perspective on life, many are caught in an internal battle as they attempt to justify life itself.

I know how it feels to sit in a meeting and have individuals in that meeting and, at that table where we sat together, never once make eye contact with me. I know how it feels to walk the halls on the job and to walk toward individual who work in the same building with me, to see them simply just walk on by without a single eye contact or a response to a "good morning."

This was bothering to me in the initial years of those experiences. But one day, I received in my heart an awesome revelation. That revelation was simply this. Those individuals that are so blatant in their dislike of others are truly hurting. They are miserable and, in some cases, have locked themselves in a prison of mistrust, hate, bigotry, and delusions for some time. Armed with this revelation, it becomes so much easier to navigate life. So what if they didn't speak? So what if they didn't notice you? So what if you are invisible to them? At a minimum, I am free. I'm free spiritually. I am free mentally. I am free financially, and I am free physically. Those are my attributes, and I will dare anyone to disarm me of them. They cannot. Can you stop the sun from shining or the rain from falling? How about stopping the day from being day and the night from being night? You may certainly try and keep trying, but your only result will be exhaustion followed by death. Why go through life being a self-imprisoned person? That's who you are when hate, bigotry, and prejudice travel through your being.

I look at my kids as they grow and the friends they have along the way, careful to lead them along a path that is positive, true, and constructive. I have seen the gradual changes in youth as the innocence of life itself becomes corrupt with the insertion of a life of hate and bigotry. I have seen how it destroys and turns innocence into deviants and derelicts. This I fight against in order to see my own children grow to be productive, contributive, and seasoned with the relevant knowledge of life, a quest for them to understand that it is the core of the man that defines him and not the superficial peripherals that is so easily speaking for this generation.

Why do personal experiences matter? Simply put, they do, and from an early age, this process of learning from experience began. Little by little, step by step, our impressions, our ideals, our passions, and our knowledge of life in general are developed and guided. We want this development to be positive, to invigorate, and to propel individuals to a better self.

Unfortunately, that is not always the case as life itself serves a cocktail of the good, the bad, and the ugly, with a side of any culture, ethnicity, or race you so choose. Is your bitterness a result of experiences along the way? Does that make everyone else in your path of life an enemy or nemesis of your cause? How do you see the value in others, the good in others, the importance in others without the clouded presence of negativity and anger?

> My dear brothers and sisters, take note of this: Everyone should be quick to listen, slow to speak and slow to become angry. (James 1:19)
>
> How beautiful it is to stay silent when someone expects you to be outraged. (Author Unknown)

Chapter 3

How can we confront situations, persons, issues, and life itself and yield something positive?

Our lives, in essence, is a communication model as we gave signals and receive signals, as we gave a word and receive a word, as we gave an action and receive an action. There is always a result, and the question really is, what result are we looking for? The saying goes, "Those who make no decision in a matter still stands guilty of making a decision to not make a decision."

How do we handle tough moments? Should we avoid it? Should we confront it? How should we confront it? And how should we avoid it? These are all questions that must be considered if we are to be effective, objective, and fair in a world filled with so much misinterpretation. Since we cannot read other people's minds, it is important to establish methods of getting correct information while making a personal effort to understand matters as we go through life. It is important to know that each individual is responsible for the communication he or she engages in.

Many of life's biases are birth from an experience of confrontation or the lack of it. To many, avoidance is just as good as elimination or the non-existence of the dilemma, but does it really?

It is important to understand that if you ignore the thing that makes you uncomfortable, it does nothing to solve the issue, remove the problem, or confirm a suspicion. In many cases, it simply exacerbates the matter—for example, you are driving along in your vehicle at night and stops at a red light. While you wait on the light to change, you glance at the vehicles stopping beside you at the light. If you had similar experiences as me, you would have noticed at least once that an individual beside you in their vehicle quickly locked their vehicle. This is noticed because you hear the click of the door latch as your traffic buddy or gal secures their vehicle. The newer cars now do this automatically for you when the vehicle begins to move. How about stepping onto an elevator with a same sex or opposite sex individual and noticing the obvious nervousness and tension they instantly exhibit? This is seen in the extra tightening of their purse or briefcase or the total avoidance and ignoring of your presence. Again many reasons can be given for these behaviors, and if you are an individual like me, you simply try not to read much into it. I am very aware of the fact that many persons have been harassed, robbed, and even have lost their lives in similar conditions. Therefore, a person exhibiting these behaviors are simply initiating a survival reaction that in most cases is an intuitive response that can be argued to be justified or rationalized. I will admit I am guilty of some of the same. I have made sure my doors were locked in some neighborhoods I drove through because I was aware of a reputation associated with that location. This is as normal as locking your doors to your home at night or closing your windows before leaving the house. All of these things we do so naturally goes back to the learned behavior or protection and survival methodology we may have obtained throughout our life.

With the majority of our communication being nonverbal, making an attempt to be keen with observation and listening, as well as understanding how we hear things, will afford us the ability to be effective communicators. Handling tough situation calls for careful thoughts and even strategy if a positive win-win result is to be achieved. This means we must consider the core of the matter first—for example, you hear from a close confidant that a coworker is always making negative and false remarks about and against you. How should you respond? First consider what may be the reasons for this behavior. Is it something you may have done or said, totally unaware of its effect on this person? What does this person have to gain by your demise? Do you have anything to gain by having a mutually respectable working relationship with this individual? Or can you simply ignore this person and their negative comments since you are sure this has zero to little impact on your life and career?

A friend of mine was faced with an interesting situation one day when an associate of his came by his place of employment and asked to speak with him for a minute. He took a few minutes away from his job to find out what was going on. To his surprise, this individual asked him directly if he was interested in his wife. My friend was totally taken back with this and managed to respond with "Are you asking me if I have a romantic interest in your wife?" The individual went on to say that he had the impression my friend was doing a lot of staring at his wife lately, and now this is leading to conflicts in their marriage. This, of course, infuriated my friend as most persons would be in a situation as this. My friend pulled his emotions together and responded by saying there was certainly some major miscommunication happening and that he was not interested in this guy's wife in any way, shape, or form. To make a long story short, it was discovered that this individual was suffering with some major insecurities personally which led to major suspicions and jealousy in his marriage at that time. This came to light after the issue was pressed aggressively by my friend. This individual came back and apologized for the incident and confessed the issues that influenced those actions. This could have resulted differently and probably for the worst, especially if my friend did not look at the entire situation and sought to have a positive dialogue with this individual.

The mind is where the majority of our endeavors, battles, dreams, visions, and heartache begins and continues to occur. It is interesting that the Bible teaches to control the thoughts first because these thoughts will turn to action which then gives a consequence. And at its end, one may be pleased, terribly saddened, afraid, or, in some cases, even lose their life. Many persons are driven not by an inherent foundation of morality and ethics but by isolated experiences which ultimately formed their outlook on many elements of society, culture, and religion.

I remembered reading an article online during the Christmas holiday that shed light on some retailer's bias with its online customers. The article shared that certain retailers were relying on information received from their customers to determine the price that customer would pay.

Interestingly it mentioned that many of the lower-income communities were being charged a higher price for items while more affluent neighborhood customers enjoyed lower prices. I found the article interesting and felt some relief knowing that I lived in a fairly good neighborhood. In fact, my wife and I had bought our home brand new. Living in the community I lived in gives me some assurance. I read several of the comments in response to the article and found some amusing, others interesting. But at times, there were those that simply stopped me with provocation of thought.

One commentator to the article wrote that he was at a store in a lower-income community and was shocked with the mob, angry, and unemployed black people clambering through the aisles.

In disgust, he left and went to a similar store in a white neighborhood where the service and atmosphere was better. For me, reading this individual's comment did not make me angry or irritate me in the least. I have had so many experiences where individuals made comments to me similar to this one that I realized that the source of these types of comments are really birth from a position of ignorance, bigotry, an isolated experience, or a corrupt heart. My peace is further strengthened by the knowledge of friends, relatives, and family I interact with who are not mobs or angry or unemployed or any of the other stereotypes that somehow gets perpetuated. I think the problem with many who find themselves in a similar place do not have the strength to simply dismiss this type of thinking, and they end up engaging it which usually offers no solution when it's all said and done. To engage ignorance is to empower it and that I deliberately fight against so I would not get sucked into that way of thinking. Are there neighborhood stores that fit this description? Of course, and can you find them in neighborhoods of different nationalities and races around the world?

Stereotyping is a prevalent component of human behavior—for example, many adhere to the notion in our society that if you are not loud, assertive, bordering on aggressive, and opinionated, you are somehow a weaker person. This then perceived weakness is attacked.

This attitude is not just an adult epidemic in our society, but we see more of it unfolding in school buildings and yards across the country. We call it *bullying* where one child exerts pressure and unwanted stress on others simply because of this perceived weakness. The fact that many of these perceived weaknesses grow up to become the leaders in societies should be enough evidence to support a shift in our thinking as a culture and society.

I remembered being at one job for over twelve years and had a fairly positive experience. My relationship with my coworkers and my supervisor(s) was positive, and I had no reasons not seeing myself employed at that job for a long time. My career started at an early age as I headed off to college, then the military, and then a civilian career without that lapse of unemployment, which many experience. I was very grateful to God for the path I was led along—that is, until I heard that my supervisor was retiring.

Upon his retirement, I found myself directly reporting to my new boss, one who saw me as too young to know anything, not smart enough to know better, and not deserving of my position at the company. Are you confused as yet? I was, too, and this was suddenly the environment I found myself in. My enjoyment of the job had become a nightmare overnight. I dreaded the thought of going into work every day and cringed whenever I was called to my new boss's office. Though the record of my job performance spoke for itself, I was suddenly being criticized, scrutinized, and at times publicly humiliated by this individual. He was arrogant in his approach and interaction with others and walked around with the air that he alone knew what the right answers were for anything. I would respond to his office time and time again to see him sitting with a stack of papers in front of him on his desk. One by one, he would begin to pull page after page from the pile with the usual "Explain this approach to me," or "Why are these items so expensive?" and the questions all followed the same tone—negative. I often drove home wondering if I was experiencing a bad dream and wishing it would be over soon.

What was it that this individual saw in me that caused him to be so offended by everything about me and everything I did? Did he have a bad experience with other black males or minority?

EVOLUTION OF LOVE AND HATE

That should not have swayed him, I thought since this was a different case, and all he had to do was look at the evidence sitting right before his eyes. I thought that would have been the simple solution to this nightmare, but that was wishful thinking on my part. This was unfolding and regardless of how hard I tried it appeared to get worse. I thought I had to do something fast, and so I made an appointment with his supervisor. His supervisor knew of the problems, especially since my case was not an isolated one but one that others were experiencing. It seemed everyone knew, but no one was willing to step forward at the time to stop what had become a problem. To make a long story short, I ended up applying and being accepted at another job, and it was a year into my new role at the new job that I got the word that that my old supervisor was finally terminated for the concerns I had tried so hard to point out.

Incidentally my experience with this matter did not leave me bitter or thinking every white person I met was racist or hateful toward me; I knew then like I know now, bad comes in all shapes, size, colors, and from every single geographical location. Failure to comprehend this simple but profound fact simply leads one down a winding trail filled with disappointment, anger, dissatisfaction, and the unfulfilled need to seek recompense and or revenge. Because of my attitude with this experience, I can look back and say that pressure at that moment in my life was the thing that propelled me to the next level of my career. My life, thank God, took a turn for the absolute best with a career that was on the right track, completion of my graduate degree, and the fulfillment of not giving up. I simply had to rise above my circumstance and not allow it to overcome and destroy me. Some may call the way I handled this situation as passive or weak. Others may say I should not have left my job. I would simply say it was a success story in the end.

A confrontation does not have to be the dreaded monster facing us. With the proper approach, you may find and understand the hidden pains and the languishing needs that so many individuals carry around. People's reaction to life is manifested in many ways, and the severity may or may not equal the level of dissatisfaction or satisfaction.

I recalled an employee I encountered several years ago in the workplace. From the first meeting, I was greeted with a hard and harsh demeanor. Her language untamed and laced with a trace of malice was the response one could always expect. The harder I tried to be polite and respectful, it seemed the worst she became, and I wondered, what on earth would have this person so bitter? Many coworkers who knew her simply stayed away and out of her way. Some returned the same angry demeanor and disrespectful gestures to her in hope of seemingly equaling the playing feel, at least so they thought.

One day, I came into work. It was an early cold morning and close to the Christmas holidays. I happened to pass by this employee and, as usual, greeted her with my usual "Good morning, how is it going?" True to fashion, the response was the same cold, uninterested reply, "Good for you."

Somehow today felt like a different day, and so I slowed my pace as I faced the individual and responded quietly and with respect, "Hmmm, not good? Sorry to hear to that."

She looked at me and replied, "Nope, this time of the year is always bad for me."

I was a bit surprised at her reply and pressed her further, "Why is that?"

"Well," she said, "several years ago my husband died on Christmas day." And she went on to share this tragic and emotional experience with me. A life that had culminated into depression and alcoholism and where everything and everyone around her would be subjected to the pain and the hurt she harbored inside. Not wanting to spoil the good thing of her, simply having a normal conversation, I listened intently with the occasional wow. I had no idea you experienced all of that.

When she was finished sharing her story, I said, "You have to trust God to help you put this behind you so that you can start living again."

She did reply, "Nope, I don't want to change." But I remembered how her attitude toward me had changed after that. She was still short to some degree but treated me more like a colleague than an enemy. Before too long, we were having regular conversations and a "Good morning" or "How is it going?" was now received with an "Okay, I'm here." How often do we or others go through life carrying the burden of isolation alone on our shoulders, thinking no one cares? Why not end it all? Too many of us are guilty of living within our sphere alone, not wanting to venture outside and not wanting anyone to venture in. This lifetime of personal, emotional, and mental isolation that ultimately cripples and destroys the soul is the reality for many. For me, I have found a release, first, in putting my faith in God and, second, valuing the support and embrace of family and friends. If our steps in life aren't bold and deliberate, then we run the chance of becoming stagnated and stuck in a rut.

Trust that your encounters along life's path will be positive, and when it is negative, simply move on with the understanding. It is their loss and not yours. Would it hurt sometimes? Yes, but I have always told myself that no one will have the power of taking my peace away from me. I may be saddened for the moment. But rest assured, I'll keep moving and getting further from that which seeks to ravish my peace, my strength, my energy, and my future.

Sadly, many allow these negative experiences to sour their destiny and stifle building meaningful relationships. They allowed that tiny measure of pain to grow into a forest of hate, ironically a forest that will eventually trap them from the world of reality, love, and hope. I remembered how my parents nurtured, encouraged, and motivated me forward in the most difficult of times. I remembered having terrible racial experiences in the workplace, and when I spoke with Dad and Mom about it, their responses were consistently the same. "Son, your destiny is bright, so don't let the negativity of others block your destiny." At times, they would refer to my bad experiences as stepping stones to my destiny. And at that time, I really didn't get it. Today I can say I truly get it.

My parents never blamed a group, a race, or an ethnicity because they understood that the seeds of life fell where they chose, but we can determine what tree grows and which ones do not. The old Eskimo folklore tells of the tribal leader who tells the young and upcoming men the story of the man who carried two wolves in his heart, one was good and the other bad. Since he could only afford to carry one, the question "Which one did he keep?" was posed, and the answer was simply, "The one you feed." Remember, if you allow your life to be trapped in a recurring cycle of negativity and bad experiences, then your actions, deeds, thoughts, and even words will begin to reflect this nurtured negativity. This hate and anger grow until it becomes easy to assault the innocent or care less for the abused. The more vivid examples in our history are those of the millions from Germany who were executed without a second thought or remorse by the hands of fascist Nazis or the thousands of blacks who were executed simply because of their race and nationality.

Remember, it is vital for you to understand that your life is truly a culmination of your actions and consequence reactions. We cannot minimize the significant importance of those daily decisions we make. How you treat and think of others around you matters. Your seemingly unimportant act today toward someone may be the defining moment in that person's life. You may never know the impact you made, positive or negative. Remember now, you have contributed to their life. What contribution would you prefer?

Recently, I was driving home from work after starting my day at four in the morning. It was an exhausting day, and as I drove home, I fought fatigue as I tried to stay awake. At a stoplight, it happened—I fell asleep and didn't realize the light had changed until I was startled awake by the honking of car horns around me. I managed to catch the light before it went red again, and as I drove off, one car behind sped around me aggressively as the driver shouted profanity and also displayed the infamous middle finger. Still tired and now shaken by the experience, I drove on.

A short time later, I stopped at the grocery store to get a few items my wife requested from me. I pulled into a parking space and stepped out of the vehicle without much thought other than to get in and out as soon as possible. As I stepped out of the car, I was face-to-face with the individual who had just a few minutes earlier hurled profanity my way. Our eyes met, and I nodded in a polite gesture toward him. It was obvious he was embarrassed or maybe even ashamed of his actions because he quickly turned away his gazed and headed to his vehicle where he got in and drove off. Think of the several possible outcomes that may have happened if either of our behaviors and actions were different. Do you think we have a part to play in the time and space we occupy? I will say resoundingly yes.

> He that has friends must first show himself friendly. (Proverbs 18:24)
>
> The first to apologize is the bravest. The first to forgive is the strongest. The first to forget is the happiest. (*The Christian Post*)

Chapter 4

From time to time, it would benefit us to self-assess our motives and our heart's content to really see what it is we are truly harboring. This assessment should be void of others' interference, no spotlight or surveys, just you facing yourself for the honest truth. These types of assessment for me are humbling partly because I chose to conduct the assessment. Others may simply dismiss any such self-assessment on the premise that they know who they are and what they believe and that is all that matters. These assessments are simply yours alone, and if you want to, you can actually learn a lot about yourself. Have you ever heard someone commit the ultimate double talk by making the statement, "I'm not a bigot. I just don't like people." You fill in the blank. This statement not only is guilty of a social double negative but actually reveals more about that person than they realized. It reminds me of an individual I once supervised. He lived in suspicion, and paranoia of everything and everyone. I met with him on many occasions to discuss ways I thought could make his outlook on life more optimistic but to no avail.

One day, he mentioned to me, "Paul, your problem is you take people at face value."

My response was simply, "Yeah, for the most part, I do because I want to give everyone the opportunity to prove to me they are either good to work with or bad to work with. If I were to simply meet someone and make the determination at that initial meeting that this person is bad or good, what good is there in pursuing anything meaningful?" Unfortunately, this is the life many live. They live lives of suspicion, mistrust, paranoia, and they fear another bad thing hiding around the corner. This is a miserable life to live, wouldn't you say? This individual eventually resigned but not before he left a trail of conflict and drama with most of the employees he had worked with. I felt sad for him.

Many persons live in this unrealistic world as they fail to see that what they say versus what's in their heart are in direct conflict, a big lie to themselves first. My youngest brother John enlightened me one day when he posted on his Facebook page the following message: "Okay, it appears that some of my Facebook associates are confused. Let me assist you then. If you want to know if you are racist, just ask yourself these questions. If you believe the skin color of a person automatically identifies what their beliefs or actions will be, you are racist. If you do not think everyone's personality, choices, ideals, and beliefs are created at a very young age by either their family, economical position in society, friends, neighborhood, education system, media, and nearby environment, then you are a racist. If you believe the color of your skin provides you with a God given advantage in life, i.e., intelligence, athleticism, cunning, strength, creativity, etc., then you are indeed a racist. Lastly if you take sides on any argument, issue, or topic solely based on skin tone, then you, my friend, are racist." I could not agree more with that statement. This is the undeniable truth of this insidious condition we label as racism or bigotry. It is simply void of the fact of the matter while solely embracing emotion. This is my baby brother echoing in essence what I am writing about without even having a conversation with me on this topic. The source of his attitude and perspective on such a critical component of human existence that is heard in his posting came from our background, our parents' philosophy on growing, and facing life and trusting God. This allows us to interact freely with all we meet as we march on toward destiny, toward success, toward our achievements.

One of the tragedies of individuals having no emotional, empathic association to an event, person, or experience allows that person to accept or justify abuse. In spite of the absent of an empathic association, the underlying fact of the matter remains true. Is there any humanistic association? This means if you have a son or a daughter, it should be easier to feel the pain of a mother or father whose son or daughter is hurt or killed. When this humanistic association does not occur, it is because the association is simply dismissed as insignificant, nonapplicable, or demonized, and this makes it easier for one to turn away from feeling obligated to help. An example of this is clearly shown in the popular media frenzy case where a white police officer fired more than five bullets to kill a black eighteen-year-old male in Ferguson Missouri. The officer testified to the grand jury that he feared for his life and stated, "The only way I can describe it is I felt like a five-year-old holding onto Hulk Hogan." He testified, "That's just how big he felt and how small I felt." This was in the physical altercation, leading to shots being fired. Once that first shot was fired, the officer testified to the jury, "He looked up at me and had the most intense aggressive face. It looked like a demon. That's how angry he looked."

I wanted to use the exact words of the officer so as not to be guilty of adding to or taking away from the fact. I have three sons and one daughter, all of whom I love dearly. I have seen them upset at each other about things and demonstrated a flood of emotion, following an outburst but not once have I associated that outburst of angry emotion as an angry demon. This is because that angry boy or girl in their temper tantrum and anger remains my son, my daughter. My wife and I have had kids over at our home, interacting with our own kids and have seen other kids act up and got angry. Let me add. Some of these kids were white. One kid even threw a metal toy at my son's head in anger over something silly. I was upset seeing my son hurt and crying, but I never once saw that kid who threw the toy as a demon.

Regardless of how you may spin this, the facts are clear; you will associate, empathize, understand those things or persons that you can relate too and want to relate to. Is it possible that the teenager killed had acted in an inappropriate way and made the officer feel threatened? Absolutely so. But when you hear no remorse or sympathy disclosed for his family's loss by the officer or many of his supporters, but instead chooses that moment to simply reiterate doing the same thing over again if given the chance, you are left wondering about the fact of the matter. It is worth noting that this eighteen-year-old who was shot was a suspect in an earlier theft, and the officer also testified that he was brutally punched through his vehicle window by the individual before firing his weapon. If all of these are true, it is clear to understand the officer being anxious and afraid for his life. Both sides of this matter require careful unbiased assessment in coming to a determination on the matter. Will there be persons who are pleased with the result of that assessment and others upset at the results? Absolutely, it is a fact of life. We can only hope that in such matters—in fact, in all matters—the assessment taken was done in the fairest possible manner with the least bit of bias contamination.

It is worth noting that every single person has the potential and has probably demonstrated this perceived exception behavior at one point in their life. It truly requires a consciousness and a deliberate effort to rise above those moments. I couple that consciousness and deliberation with my faith in God because I'll be the first to admit that there are times when you don't feel like being understanding or compassionate. I just want retribution and revenge, but what road does that take one on? Many experts, particularly in anger management, would admit many of the decisions made in anger are regrettable ones. It is, therefore, important for one to understand the significance of self-control and restraint. It is an attribute that can be utilized in a marriage or in the workplace or even in an intense negotiation in order to achieve a positive outcome.

Today many in our society have adapted a selfish position which has been glorified with the modern-day vernacular individualism. This justified approach to what was considered and seen decades ago as selfish and destructive is now hailed as a positive character and a social trait for individuals to possess. This drive for individualism is so strong that those who veer off that road becomes isolated, ostracized, and at times criticized as being weak. Many fail to understand that in spite of individual fortitude, we are very much in need of each other's support.

Visit a nursing home or elderly-care facility like I have had the opportunity to do, and you will see that many of these aged men and women are there lonely and sad. Many of them cannot remember the last time a loved one stopped by to visit them. For some, their only recollection now balances on the memories of that last holiday visit from a love one. In spite of their younger and more vibrant life as they commanded their career and life forward, they were now confined, aged, and lonely in a facility or even a room. Individualism has long left their repertoire of ambitions only now to be replaced with a longing for friendship, communication, and the ultimate desire to be loved and to have companion by their side. This image, as sad as it is, remains a very true and common occurrence in our society today. The cycle of selfishness and individualism continues on in those younger generations as they too march toward a life of isolation and loneliness. My siblings and I have made the commitment that we would rather not allow our parents to live their elderly years in such an environment even if it requires a sacrifice.

Our honesty with ourselves first is where it truly begins. We can make statements and act in certain ways depending on the time, place, or circumstance, and most would have no idea really of our intent and motives. Only you can make that individual assessment of your motives. For years, we as a country have elected presidents, all white; and though we have debated the difference in positions and policy. Race has never been an issue for any of the millions of Americans voting, so we thought until Obama became president. Many had simply dismissed the very notion that anyone other than a Caucasian individual had the ability to be president of this great country. That thought was unconscious. Many, even during the campaigning cycle, as the polls showed him having a commanding lead over other candidates, simply dismissed this as a passing anomaly. No efforts were made to stop him, and no divisive attacks were being levied at him. Of course, this all changed overnight when he became the democratic candidate to run for president. From that moment and after his election to president, many hearts and inner thought of persons began erupting to the surface. The once dormant bigotry, stereotypes, and prejudices now were unleashed and untamed. Many even in the halls of congress and the senate and other areas of the highest levels of government openly jeered him with derogatory names and racist comments. They had felt cheated, caught off guard, and were angry and wanting revenge with venom. Most of us would remember then senate minority leader making the statement that their (republicans) goal was to make this president a one-term president and wanted him to fail. The public now saw a systematic approach by the opposing party to derail and obstruct everything this president attempted to do, even when many of those same policies and initiatives he presented were promoted in the past by them.

Prior to this period, many would have argued that they were anything but prejudice or racist. It was well hidden, and frankly speaking, there was nothing really around to fully awaken that sleeping giant. That is nothing until the election of Barack Obama as president of the United States. For these individuals, the thought alone sickened them as they experienced the symptomatic stages of loss, following a devastating news that started with denial that this is actually happening and not just a bad dream. Soon the bad dream became obviously real, and anger and resentment that kill set in. The next process of bargaining or rationalizing came sweeping in as many attempted to justify what had happen. Many thought the country did not take the election serious, or all the black people voted so it made it easier for him. The list of excuses went on. This bargaining in order to justify their rage grew as they targeted the president's reelection. They were confident it would not happen again. After all, they were now more vigilant and ready. But to no avail, Obama was granted another term by the majority of Americans. This still was not enough to satisfy the rage burning inside those individuals, and they soon erupted into a depressed state of seeing everything around their world and the country as "going to hell." Acceptance, the last stage in this process, is the stage that they refuse to accept. This will power simply will continue to fuel their disdain at the very thought of a minority being in the white house.

These realities are the fact of the matter that must be dealt with at the heart level. It is easy to conceal a matter deep in the recesses of one's heart as long as that emotional tight string is not disturbed. Once a disturbance of that emotional tight string occurs, then the eruption of what lie dormant rushes to the surface to be exposed. This again demonstrating the biblical text that out of the abundance of the heart, the mouth speaks. It is time to assess what is really hidden deep in the recesses of our heart. As in the case of Obama's election, those that deny it are attacking reality itself. The reality is that an election to president would not have happened without the support given by members of all groups—whites, blacks, Hispanics, and others all contributing to his election.

> Above all, love each other deeply, because love covers a multitude of sins. (1 Peter 8:4)
> Forgiveness is the final form of love.
> (Reinhold Niebuhr)

Chapter 5

You know one of the most interesting things about denying something is that it usually has no consequence on the reality or fact of the matter. I can deny all day long on the existence of the wind. The trees will continue to bustle in its presence and is unhindered by anyone's opinion of the matter. The same can be said about many issues we face in our society from homelessness, hunger, greed, bigotry, and, of course, racism. Its denial means nothing for or against it, and all that is left in the path of denial is a trail of reality.

My wife and I once bought a rocking horse toy for our one-year-old son, and he loved it. Shortly after getting that rocking horse home, I noticed my oldest, who was five at the time, was also sneaking a ride on it. Several times I would reiterate to him that it was not the same for him because it was created for a smaller weight load. He never really believed us and would continue to steal a ride when he could. One day, when I arrived home, he greeted me with a fairly solemnly expression that instantly told me something was wrong. Before I could say anything, he started off, "Dad, I broke the rocking horse. I didn't mean to do it." I was upset as you can imagine but used the opportunity to teach him about action and consequences, as well as obedience. His denying of the fact of the rocking horse's weight limit didn't give it an extra boost to support his weight. It simply broke. I find myself thinking many times as I observe and hear of situations or experiences exhibited and demonstrated in our society. Does something have to break before reality sinks in? This question is not asked because I am anticipating a cure, a fix-it-all and ultimately, utopia. We can instead seek solutions that can minimize our ships of life from sinking and constantly being in a state of emergency while we scramble to implement rescue, recovery, and repair missions.

You have to understand that the difference between a ship that is sailing along on top of the sea without taking in water and sinking and a ship that is riddled with holes and sinking fast is not the sea itself going away but simply the construction of the ship and its safety features at its disposal. I muse when I hear persons saying racism and bigotry is no longer around, but it is just as baffling when I hear others saying that nothing has changed. The truth is, there has been a tremendous amount of changes that has occurred in our society over the past several decades, but the work never ends. It is necessary for us as a species, to continue to collectively seek solutions, innovations, and methods that will enhance our lives and progress our future. The alternative to that is we will be like other dynamic civilizations that came before us. They are simply a historic story and a recollection with no one left to add credence to their prior existence apart from the records, physical ruins, and artifacts gathered. If you study the Ten Commandments, whether you are religious or not, you will see that laws that were created, at its core, was not to simply infuse dos and don'ts into a society and culture, but they were anchored in those foundational attributes for a culture's endurance and existence.

The Ten Commandments embodies some core fundamentals which when taken away from a society, only leads to chaos, degradation, and ultimately, destruction. Looking closely at the first three commandments or laws, we can draw the modern-day parallel for a better understanding.

1. *You will have no other God before me.* This was not based on the philosophy of a culture with many gods but on the understanding that we serve and embrace one God. Anything else placed before him violates this law. How we can place other things before him is the question one may ask. If we place more importance on our career, our money, our hobbies and activities than we give to our servitude to Christ Jesus the creator, then we are in violation. As we look around in society today, do you see the over

indulgence and focus on all these things? It is no wonder why man's occupation has been coined so well, the rat race. Look at a city dump or garbage-infested back alley, and you will see rats running back and forth driven by a need to get more, survive, and procreate. That is their sole purpose until one day, they die. Not the life I want to live, do you? I'm assured of life beyond this human flesh and blood. If you are not a Christian, then you probably see this section of the Ten Commandments as something foreign but keep reading because history is dotted with examples of what was once seen as crazy only to be one day seen as something innovative and essential to our future.

2. *You will not create and worship any images.* Simply put, when we allow anything to become gods in our lives, we are unconsciously choosing to make the remaining area of our life less significant. Looking at some of the other areas in life that generally take the second, third, or no-importance position, we will begin to see things as love and caring for each other, forgiveness and encouragement, support and empathy for the less fortunate, and last but not the least, the ability to treat others the way we would love to be treated. Sadly many persons simply focus on that thing or person that will benefit them, period.

At its core, they do not care if it means stepping on or evening killing to get that satisfaction. That is their singular focus. Some persons care more for their pet than a fellow human being and have no shame in vocalizing this. It is sad to see and hear of persons dying and not having a single person present by their side or claiming their bodies. Some have lived an entire life in isolation blocked from truly seeing and experiencing humanity's best. Understand that loving your pet is not the issue here or focusing on a career path or even having a dream. The issue begins when each of these things becomes more important than our cultivated relationship and intimacy with each other. Study divorce statistics, and you will see that the majority of the causes were rooted in some form of selfishness. Somewhere along the line, a spouse chose to make career, money, extra marital affairs, and other things more important to them than their spouse. They then make the declaration, "Things just grew apart between us," or the famous celebrity line, "We have irreconcilable differences." In other words, we have our focus and goals that will continue to be important to each of us, and it doesn't matter that those goals and those focus places our spouse in a lesser place of value.

Now, I am in no way Mr. Perfect, but I often take a step back when I see my wife upset, particularly at me, and I try hard to see what angle she may be viewing all of it through. Many times, after taking this time to reflect, I actually begin to soften up which really becomes a catalyst to reconciliation. How can we compromise if there is no letting go? How can we love when we choose to simply hate? And how can we experience the joy of giving if we are only bent on receiving? Like a carefully calibrated weight scale, life in balance yield so much more than we can even imagine. It is not good enough to simply be good, we must be conscious of the fact that our good can become great if we open up to having the right persons around us. Think of well-known athletes with all of their accomplishments and statistics. It is clear that they did not do it as a one-man team. In fact, it took the collaborative efforts of other team members contributing in some ways. I have seen many a great athlete never winning any championship largely in part because they were surrounded by teammates who failed to contribute their part. As you know, all of the individual greatness tends to fade when that team ends the season without that coveted championship.

Unfortunately, many in our society are behaving daily like the "me alone" athlete or the selfish spouse. They don't care what or who is affected by their actions or words as long as it satisfies their immediate desire to be recognized, validated, or revenged. This type of thinking allows and accommodates behavior and actions that ordinarily would not be accepted in general but because it is perpetuated by isolated, victimized perspective, they can easily condone those extreme actions or behavior. One man's response to being involved in a malicious and barbaric style execution of another man when asked why he did it was, "I guess I was there with a group of persons who all were hyped up on doing this." How empty was that response to the taking of a life? Yet we see time and time again actions and words being delivered with no more than an idea, a thought, without proof or valid reason. This unfortunately is too often the end to the worthless journey in life so many choose to cuddle.

Like the child replying to my son's question as to why he thinks black people are bad, "Because they just are," this now becomes the doctrine and ideology that child will embrace, nurture, and ultimately seek to reinforce over her life. This then becomes reinforced and solidified to the point where it may eventually spiral out of control. For my child, the correct nurturing and development by my wife and me leaves them in a better position to face a world that may be rooted in bigotry and hate.

Persons who operate from this base are never satisfied; they speak a good game and give a good impression that they are enjoying and actually loving this life of bigotry, hate, and vitriol, but the truth of the matter is, they are simply inflicting pain time and time again into their own lives.

They are hoping that with each incident and each mean action, they could get relief. The drug addict thought the same thing earlier into his or her experience only to realize after the fact that they had become a slave to a divisive and destructive force whose ultimate desire is but to steal their dreams, kill their future, and destroy their lives. At one point, this road becomes close to impossible to turn around and so continuing the journey is the only option they are left to embrace all the way to their demise.

From time to time, our nation sees some of the pointless results of a life spent nursing this sick perspective. Year after year, Dylan Roof fueled his thoughts and spirit with hate as he consumed volumes of information that were tailored made to anger him and to justify and validate his hate, his bigotry, and the information he was fed. Friends saw the demise occurring. Others noticed that the humanity in him was slipping away and was being replaced with emptiness. This journey only led him to commit the heinous act of murder when he walked into a congregation and opened fire, killing eleven innocent victims. His intent was still denied with the anticipation of igniting a race war that failed to occur. All the hate, all the planning, all the bigotry, and all the lives he took only led to one thing—more solidarity, more love, more courage and grace. For him, it was the sentence to the remainder of his natural life of seeing the sea of love and grace and mercy and forgiveness growing to envelope and engulf his hate. He lost.

Matthew Sheppard, the man who was brutally killed in Wyoming because of his sexuality and left to die an agonizing death alone in the middle of nowhere, also ignited support and solidarity that stifled the men who perpetrated this hate and bigotry. When individuals allow themselves to be consumed by all of the things that can so easily cloud our judgment, they become oblivious to reality and they sink into a world of suspicion, mystery, conspiracy theory, and death. The wind is blowing; don't trust me just feel it.

Reality doesn't have to be the large surprising smackdown in our life. It simply can become a rudder that guides us along life's journey(s). I tend to think of it this way—becoming aware of the dangers of the rattlesnakes allows us to not walk right into or on it. Once we hear that rattle from its tail and then spot the snake itself, we are then able to pull from our understanding of the snake and avoid placing ourselves in further danger. Imagine not knowing of the rattle snake or its venomous ability, one would simple walk into a life-threatening situation.

> Love prosper when a fault is forgiven, but dwelling on it separates close friends. (Proverbs Chapter 17:9)
> When you choose to forgive those that hurt you, you take away their power.

Chapter 6

If you are old enough, you will recall the days when you are out of school for the summer how much fun life was. You played a lot and enjoyed the big things, like vacation and weekend getaway trips, to the small things, like poking at bugs or anthills in the yard. Very soon we entered into the world of adulthood and our ability to relax and enjoy life seems to have screeched to a halt. Again for Christianity, the idea here is to set aside a day to relax. Focus on the important things in your life. Hopefully God, family, and friends are those important things.

Push the pause button on your life and understand that even as a business owner, you can continue to make money and probably be more successful when you begin to acknowledge that these more important things in life will continue to tick and be spoken of long after you, the money, and other material things are gone.

Today the notion of a day of rest is more of a bygone era in memory that we can reminisce on from time to time. Businesses have increased and maintained their operations 24/7 Sunday through Saturday, and employees are working longer days and more hours as together we work at delivering and obtaining the good life. None of the money, prestige, and material possession matters when you are facing death in the face. The thing that matters at that time is being surrounded by those who love you and are assured that you are going to a better place.

With this thought in mind, how can one live a life of hate and focus on so much that does not matter? Meanwhile, they are neglecting and abandoning the true relevance of their lives and existence.

I saw a photo shown to me by a friend of mine of a group of white men, maybe twenty-five or so, assembled together in a yard for a photo shoot. Some were smiling and others laughing. Some held their heads high in pride of their accomplishment. As I stared at the photo, I felt a sadness as the full photo view became evident. Hanging above this group of happy and excited men was a black man, dead. His neck was broken from the noose around that was suspended from a tree branch above. His arms were tied behind his back. He looked beaten and rugged as evident by the torn shirt and pants he wore. His feet were bare as he hung there from that tree, dead.

I thought how another human being could demonstrate this type of malicious and painful actions without remorse. Unfortunately, before that thought left, I knew why. Men, women, boys, or girls who are void of any relational or humane identity with something or someone can easily perform an execution. It would be no difference from a cow or chicken in a slaughterhouse yet even the chicken and cows have advocates petitioning to stop their killing. I have also seen video footage of black men gunning down other black men all in the sicken ideology of gang affiliation without realizing that this type of affiliation comes back full circle to a desensitizing and dehumanizing that prevents them from seeing the value in themselves and others.

This lack of reflection on the truly important things and persons becomes chronic in its effect.

Persons begin to lack the ability to see others equally, love others the way they want to be loved and respected and understood. It places them in an isolation chamber of life, only identifying with their box and circle and never daring to step out. This approach only produces selfishness, but the sad thing about this selfishness is that it always finds a way to blame someone else or something else for its demise and sadness. It fails to step up and assume the responsibility needed. The men in the examples I referenced with the killing were all selfish in that moment, occupied with their lives, their needs, their wants, and never had the time to stop and see how isolated and alone they truly were. That is what hatred and bigotry does. It steals, destroys, and kills any and everything in its path without remorse.

EVOLUTION OF LOVE AND HATE

Now the first four commandments probably needed some explanation as I have given, but the remaining instructions are fairly comprehensible. It does not take a rocket scientist or an astrophysicist to clarify what honor your mother and father means. It is reprehensible to see an elderly man or woman being mistreated and disrespected by anyone. That abuse then takes on an almost sacrilegious tone when the abuser is a child and more damning if the child is related to the individual. This type of abuse goes hand in hand with incest and the likes because it violates the natural order of our existence. When any natural order is violated, it will usually result in a disaster. The disaster in the case of one who is abusive to a parent is for that person ending up with a life ahead with equal or more woes. This is such a dynamic commandment that it gives a reward for those who adhere to it. That reward says, "That your days may be long upon the land." Length of years added for honoring your parents is a good thing for one to look forward to.

My dad, whom I loved dearly, passed away at the age of seventy-seven. His full and joyful years were blessed with the opportunity to witness the marriage of his children and to enjoy the fellowship and interaction of his grandkids, all twenty-five of them at the time of his death. He lived a long, enjoyable, and rewarding life. He honored his parents; and though I never met my grandfather who passed away early, I knew Dad loved him and Grandma both. He always made references to his early years as a child and the support and love he experienced from his parents.

This intricate string in our lives and in our society of honoring parents, respecting adults, and those in authority strengthens societies and cultures. When this string is severed and compromised and violated, we see the resulted demise in our society, individuals wanting to do and say what they want to do and say. There is no consideration for others but rather a pervasiveness of selfishness that seems to overshadow our lives. I recalled looking at a video someone recorded of a group of young men, probably in their teens and early twenties, physically assaulting an elderly gentleman. It broke my heart as I watched this and was even more horrified as I heard on the video the laughter and cheering that accompany the assault.

These young men were callous and desensitized. If they only had the ability to imagine their own father or grandfather being treated this way, then maybe that would have compelled them to halt the attack. Sadly some of these acts are also happening where the victim's assailant is a family member. The other side of this is, what if this behavior was a behavior that was passed down from generation to generation. This environment for these individuals would only be the familiar demised generation of degradation and dishonoring of the elderly, the parents, and those in authority. The remaining biblical laws are also significant when studied in context. We can see the distinct correlation to many of societal inadequacies directly being affected by the failure to adhere to these laws or commandments.

> For just as each of us has one body with many members; these members do not have the same functions. (Roman 12:4)
> Everyone in the boat should be concern about a leak suddenly discovered; for all will be going under if that leak isn't fixed.

Chapter 7

There is a fact to the assembling of shared interest, values, and other things. This factor holds true to race, ethnicity, culture, nationality, faith, and more. To deem these natural humanistic characters as bad or somewhat faulty is to look at life through inhibited vision. Having said that, there is a balance to life that is similar to everything elsewhere; and when that balance is changed, the results is often more negative than positive. By now, you are trying to figure out where I am going with this thought. If you go to any community or neighborhood or even churches, you will see that folks of same mind-set usually end up hanging together. Race does play into that selection process but is not the only determinant for this type of congregating. I have non-black friends who, in our initial meeting, were very distant and not wanting to develop any friendship beyond the meet and greet, "See you later." Many even confided in me after the fact that their initial behavior and attitude toward me was primarily predicated on an ideology or stereotype. Many even would make that unpopular declaration, "You're not like other."

Depending on our environment, we will identify and align with those that we feel more comfortable around. But again, that is not always the case. After all, the church is one of the most segregated places in our nation on Sundays with black churches and white churches and Hispanic churches. I have even attended churches where I felt isolated sitting in a sea of people. Of all the places, you would expect this type of isolation; some would say the church should be the last. I would agree and add that it would be the case if the church was truly filled with people of like mind, living fully according to principles and doctrine of the faith, but neither is that the case. Only those willing to step outside of their comfort zone and are willing to leave those crippling stereotypes and inbred ideology at home would be able to experience the glory of life without boundaries. I have lived in Texas, Oklahoma, Colorado, South Carolina, and Wyoming. I visited over twenty states in the United States, visited several countries in the Caribbean, and I was born and raised in Guyana, South America. Many times when I speak to many of my friends living on the East Coast of the United States or in the northwest, I sometimes hear reluctance to come and visit the West. They are more comfortable with their environment and often see elsewhere through lens of stereotypes and others' experiences. The same can be said about many living in the West and other areas; they, too, are reluctant to venture into other unfamiliar territory and are comfortable staying where they are. We have grown accustomed to embracing the familiar and shunning the unfamiliar, and that is regardless of whether or not it can benefit us or not. This character trait we all have allows for safety, security, relationship, and even intimacy; but taken beyond the balance of its boundaries, we can and will continue to see negativity being birth.

Jim Jones was a religious ideologue that became disillusioned and misguided. He transformed himself from a religious leader that guided and led persons to God to one who began to see himself as a god. When this spiritual evolving began, he ultimately isolated the hundreds of people following him from all associates, including relatives, and eventually forced them to drink poison in committing a mass suicide. He himself committed suicide. This sad situation really reflects and symbolizes the lives of so many people on a daily basis. Persons who have grown to rely on themselves and completely discrediting the significance and relevance of God the creator have traveled this road of self-sustaining, self-fulfilling, and self-reliance until they realize that it only leads to a dead end. I do believe that one cannot live a fulfilled life without the inclusion of Christ, yet many seemingly intelligent individuals who ridicule and downplay the significance of religion as a crutch for the weak, are themselves naive and brain-washed.

EVOLUTION OF LOVE AND HATE

How could one think that any living species on this planet, with all of its intricacies and advance central nervous system, is simply a result of random and chaotic concoction of nature? In that case, I think I will go and sit by city dump and hope my dream car is created in and from the heap of trash. Now the intelligence of man, coupled with the reality and recognition that there is a God, will allow one to embrace elements of science that are truly scientific and will allow him to discard those elements of science that are based and constructed solely on the premise of untested theoretical reasoning. This same untested theoretical reasoning is employed daily in the minds of many who choose to follow blindly an ideology that promises them more intelligence, better lives, and supremacy. Some so deeply embraced this notion that with the election of Barack Obama, a black man, becoming the president of the United States and leader of the free world, hate, bigotry, and decades of systematic emotional, societal, and economical programming, only allowing them to see a pejorative, the *n* word. With God's help, it is easy for a person to begin to change their thinking and perspective, but it will have to be with God's help, a spiritual surgery of the heart. I believe spiritual surgery of the heart is the only cure to remove the years of programming many live with from day to day. A social program or club or regulations and policies enacted by the state or federal government will never affect a heart to change.

If we take a look at the position held by the leadership conference, which is referenced as the nation's premier civil-right and human-right coalition, their position on this matter is reflected in their statement on affirmative action. It reads,

> As President Lyndon Johnson said in 1965, "You do not take a person who, for years, has been hobbled by chains and liberate him, bring him up to the starting line of a race and then say you are free to compete with all the others, and still just believe that you have been completely fair."

President Johnson's speech eloquently stated the rationale behind the contemporary use of affirmative action programs to achieve equal opportunity, especially in the fields of employment and higher education. The emphasis is on opportunity: affirmative action programs are meant to break down barriers, both visible and invisible, to level the playing field and to make sure everyone is given an equal break. They are not meant to guarantee equal results but instead proceed on the common-sense notion that if equality of opportunity were a reality, African Americans, women, people with disabilities, and other groups facing discrimination would be fairly represented in the nation's workforce and educational institutions. (civilrights.org)

Though this statement attempts to bring some gravitas to issues of changing someone's heart and mind, it remains a divisive and often challenged issue in our modern day with a clear divide for those in favor or against this issue of affirmative action. Though this book is not about the particular issue of affirmation action. I used this small example to show how our perspective and thoughts on issues can be so solidified over our lifetime that a change in perspective can be downright challenging. When this change in thinking occurs, it has to be predicated on the heart and emotion of one being changed for it to be true and authentic.

After all, we have all heard persons simply making the statement "I'm not this or that," or "I don't think I treat others differently," when in actuality we may know of, heard them, and even seen them demonstrate some of these same acts and expression of prejudice and bigotry. Somehow these individual simply thinks their verbal declaration is all it takes to position them with the right optics of being seen in one light versus another. Others willingly and consciously would take this approach knowing that to truly show their true feelings on the matter may bring them some unwanted attention, ridicule, or repercussion. Can you see why I have made it a point to say that policies, and regulations, though necessary, does not bring about the type of change we truly would like to see? That type of change must be from the source, the heart, and only then can the change be legitimized.

It reminds me of the teenage daughter of some close friends of ours, who happens to be Caucasian, making the statement on the day Mr. Obama was elected. "Now that Barack Obama is elected president, all these people complaining about racial issues should now stop." As you can imagine, I simply smiled. She had no understanding that this issue transcended the optics of a black man's election to presidency of the Unites States of America and would somehow instantaneously erase and transform hearts of hate, bigotry, and the perspectives of superiority. Thinking on this matter superficially, you can easily see how many may simply process that legitimately. When discussing the reality of human relationships, change can only be legitimate when it is generated from the level of the heart.

I recalled a story my father mentioned often when he preached on man's stubborn nature. He references a boy who attended an English private boarding school. The practice was when addressing the headmaster that a child should stand and remain standing until the conversation was over before sitting. Well, this particular young boy would always refuse to stand and address his teacher until one day, the teacher was overcome by frustration in the child's disrespect. He ordered him to stand or be immediately expelled. The boy slowly rose to his feet and with arms clasp tightly across his chest, he muttered softly but loud enough to be heard "I'm standing but I'm still sitting on the inside." Many in our society go through life as this child being force to comply with policies, regulation, laws, and other societal governances while vehemently still defiant to their core.

Under this condition, it is only a matter of time before individuals or groups become so saturated that an eruption beyond their control come bursting to the surface. When that occurs, the usual outcry, as we have seen in society, is shock and, more often, surprise. We would hear a statement like "I never thought he or she was like this or capable of such an act." It serves to remind us over and over again that the saying, "You cannot judge a book by its cover," really has some validity to it. Are you a slave to your environment of familiarity? Or are you strong enough to forge a path forward that is a culmination of shared, learned experiences of the highs and lows of your life?

The ability to rise up against a sea of sitters, to swim against the ever so prevailing strong current, in setting an identity that is true to self, God, and others. This ability will yield fruits you could not imagine having without this type of transformational thinking and awareness. For those familiar with the Bible, one verse in Philippians chapter 4, verse 8 reads,

> Finally, brothers, whatever is true, whatever is honorable, whatever is just, whatever is pure, whatever is lovely, whatever is commendable, if there is any excellence, if there is anything worthy of praise, think about these things.

This really adds credence to the fact that regardless of the front one presents, the true self will eventually show itself. If we look at the many still circulating in the dating scene, we will see this familiar presenting of a facade versus the real self.

It is a period of bliss where all is well. All appears perfect with our date not being able to do any wrong. Of course, this changes over time as we see that person's true identity and character being revealed. This revealing may be positive or negative. In most cases, the real self, emotions, addictions, and simple character traits lay somewhat dormant. This masquerading can only continue for a limited time before that proverbial button is pushed to reveal truth, and that truth is the real emotions, the real character and thoughts, and the real responses to life itself. This is so common that many enter into marriage without an awareness of the reality; their entire courtship and romance were all predicated on a lie and a pretense that faded shortly thereafter. Even in dating someone with the prospect of marriage, one must take into consideration what thoughts, emotions, and experiences are truly governing this individual. Finding out this information before marriage certainly helps one to make that decision of whether or not this is a relationship worthy of sticking with all the way to marriage.

>The one who does not love does not know God for God is love. (1 John 4:8)
>Forgiveness is unlocking the door to set someone free and realizing you were the prisoner. (Author Unknown)

Chapter 8

The Bible or good book as some prefer to call it reads in John chapter 8 that you will know the truth and the truth will set you free. This freedom being referenced here goes beyond a mere physical liberation but truly addresses the liberation and freedom that one can experience in themselves as a result of accepting the truth. Many individuals who committed crimes and who may have gotten away with it have been so plagued by their own self-awareness of the crime that they would eventually confess to someone. I can only submit that this self-confession came as a result of that turmoil occurring inside of them. This internal turmoil exists as a result of many things. I have simply used one as an example, but many persons live with thoughts and experiences that haunt them silently with every day that they live. Many find liberation from this self-turmoil only after confessing and acknowledging that which is tormenting them. Another component of confession involves an individual recognizing that issue—in this case, prejudice—as wrong. After all, there is no confession, especially of wrongdoing, when I simply view my actions as acceptable, good, justified, or appropriate to a cause.

It is with this understanding that the issue of bigotry and prejudice should be viewed and discussed. This is so because many see their prejudicial actions, attitude, and words as acceptable, good, justified, and appropriate to their upbringing or ideals. The other component to this embraced set of values or ideal may also lie in the reality that where there is no value, as in humanity's dignity, then abuse, misuse, and discrediting is easy to be perpetuated. The Bible also chimed in on this concept in more than one location. One location in the book of Luke chapter 6 reads, "Do unto others as you would have them do unto you." Any sound minded person reading this would have no problem with the fact that they themselves would like to be treated fairly with kindness, with understanding, love, etc. In spite of this clear understanding and interpretation, something happens in an individual's mind when they relate to others who may be different from them. These differences may be in areas as race, ethnicity, gender, education, and other determinant factors. If there is not a shared center to persons they are interacting with, then negativity toward those individuals, in many instances becomes unconsciously acceptable, good, justified, and fittingly appropriate to their ideals.

The truth is radical in its delivery, and whether you agree with the truth or not, it remains the truth. We may disagree that gravity exists; but if we jump from a rooftop, our beliefs have no effect on the results. The truth takes over, and you will be falling to the ground with or without your belief in gravity. It is this truth that I concluded that persons who are bigoted and prejudice really do hate themselves. After all, if I see a child being abused and mistreated, my reaction will be one of sympathy for that child and anger toward the perpetrator. Why the sympathy and anger? Simple, I can imagine my own child being abused and mistreated, and that thought would be painful. I can imagine myself being abused and mistreated and that thought is not one that makes me happy. To think persons can stand by and watch others being mistreated and abused really brings us face to face with a quote from the Bible which says, "The heart of man is desperately wicked. Who can know it?"

When my nine-year-old son comes home after spending some time at a friend's home and tells me, "Dad, when Jim and I were walking to the park, someone drove by and yelled from their car 'Nigger!'" As a parent, you are staring the truth in the face, and you need to respond.

My response was simple, "Son, as long as he did not physically harm you, ignore his ignorance. They hate because they are lacking something inside and needing help." The profound truth that we will face in our life and society and the world is that prejudice, bigotry, and bad things will always exist around us. Those operating without a moral compass that I find in serving Jesus Christ will fall victim to this cauldron, and like a whirlpool in a large body of water, they will be sucked in closer, closer, until—oops—too late down they go spiraling into the depth of oblivion, a sad place to be indeed.

The resounding fact of truth is that it truly stands uncontested and real in a world filled with counterfeit, dishonesty, lies, and misrepresentation. Czeslaw Milosz, Lithuanian author, wrote that "in a room where people unanimously maintain a conspiracy of silence, one word of truth sounds like a pistol shot." It is imperative that those of us who discover the divisiveness of bigotry and hate must deploy the "pistol shot" of truth in defending and protecting the innocent while being the tool that offers a rescue to those caught in the whirlpool of unconscious oblivion.

This societal cancer can spread and destroy lives, homes, and society when left unchecked. It festers and enlarges while annihilating its entire path. It should remind us all of the atrocities of the Nazi regime on its quest to create that pure race with the execution of millions of innocent Jewish men, women, and children. The bigotry and hate should remind us of the atrocities committed by former Ugandan president, Idi Amin, who deployed mass execution of all who dare stand in his way to remain in power. This rage against humanity was demonstrated to the world on many levels and platform and unfortunately sanctioned or allowed by many societies. In our own great country of America, our history also displays a dismal pass of hate and bigotry as we saw thousands of black men, women, and children suffer unbelievable atrocities without the intervention of anyone while receiving the approval and support of these atrocities by presidents, farmers, and preachers alike. How any of these generation of people survived can only be answered as we study those who rose to stand against the wrong they saw, those who rose to shatter the silence by firing that round of truth and daring to force others to face the truth of their lives, their actions, and their heart.

Many individuals today do not realize they harbor biases in the recesses of their hearts; and without an incident or event occurring to awaken it, they could go for years operating under the blanket of being open-minded, and free of hate and prejudice. When triggered by an event or incident, things simply flow out with veracity, leaving all who witness it without the shadow of a doubt that here was hate and prejudice and evil being demonstrated. Evil of prejudice and hate goes beyond the walls of race and ethnicity. It travels in the realms of bias and personal affiliations. Think of recent events in our history involving racial matters, and you will see persons rallying to support both side of the issue regardless of the facts. This type of unconscious support thrown in support of a cause or association truly solidifies the fact that individuals, regardless of their race, ethnicity, or social echelon, will identify with that which appears more identifiable. The stunning irony is seen too often as you analyze case by case to see how support can easily switch from supporting to opposing and from opposing to supporting a position based solely on who they are supporting or opposing.

In case after case, the relevance has little to no effect on what is being supported or opposed and primarily on who is being supported. I am black, yet I do not run to defend a black drug dealer's behavior or other societal negatives committed by blacks. If ingrained prejudices exist, then sound, rational reasoning is simply out of mind in most cases. Instead, actions are fuel and perpetuated by a stereotype, an experience and or an event that is allowing them to simply make generalized judgments. Many individuals will read this book and make disparaging remarks about me and some of the material written, but again it has absolutely nothing to do with changing the truth.

The truth is that there is prejudice and bigotry, and we all possess levels of biases. But the degree of our biases and its control on our actions really determines the differentiation between normal and prejudice.

My wife and I work diligently to educate and inform our kids of the realities of life outside of our home; and in spite of my initial anxiety with the birth of our first child, I am confident my wife and I are instilling the right dose of information and education into them to make them balance and productive members of society. This was demonstrated one day when my kids returned home from swimming lessons at the local recreational center; and Jasmine, my daughter, eight years old at the time, came to me and said, "Dad, you would be proud of Israel today?" Now Israel is our third child and second son and, at this time, had just turned five. Jasmine continued, "During our swimming lessons, this other kid pointed to Israel and said, "Why are you black?"

Israel replied, "Because God made me that way."

The little girl continued, "Well, God only likes white people."

Israel again responded, "No, God loves everybody."

I was still somewhat shocked to be hearing this coming from a four or five-year-old child, and I asked Israel directly if this was true. Of course, he answered, "Yes, Dad, it is true." Imagine the millions of thoughts going through our minds as parents. *Where did she get that from? And how extreme is this type of information fed to her?* After all, children are like young seedlings with which you can bend and twist to whatever desired configuration you choose. As this seedling grows, that bending and adjusting becomes increasingly more difficult until one day you simply have what you have.

Until we individually begin to assess our lives and examine the recesses of our hearts, we will continue to live in the box of which simply makes us the most comfortable while we will ostracize and even hide the box that makes us uncomfortable. We are, indeed, products of our environment, but that does not mean we cannot force ourselves to step outside of our own perspective and world to see and experience life beyond the boundaries.

> Love prospers when a fault is forgiven, but dwelling on it separates close friends. (Proverbs 17:9)
>
> Forgiveness is the best form of love, it takes a strong person to say sorry and even stronger person to forgive. (Unknown Author)

Chapter 9

As a parent, one of the most difficult things to see and experience is seeing one of my kids do something wrong and then trying hard to dodge the responsibility once that wrong is discovered.

There is something sinister about individuals who hide from their responsibilities and instead chose to blame someone else. Unfortunately our society has an unlimited amount of examples of persons choosing to blame others for their problems, their wrongs, their mistakes, their failures but never once owning up to the fact that, at one point, personal responsibility is a necessity. Though there are some conditions that can influence actions, we must be able to rise above our experience to steer and control our actions and our responses. I love quoting Charles Swindoll's poem, "The Attitude." For in it, he really summarizes a key component to success in the following sentences: "I am convinced that life is 10 percent what happens to me and 90 percent how I react to it, and so it is with you. We are in charge of our attitudes!"

What a true insight on our experiences and our responses to those experiences. It is true that we should not deny the impact experiences and environment has on us individually, but we should allow our responses and focus to be one that fuels us to something better, our destiny. Instead of this positive perspective and response, many succumb to a response and a focus that is destructive. I am thinking of the art which demonstrates perseverance and never giving up in its display of a blue heron with a frog in its beak while the frog maintains an oxygen starved grip on the neck of that heron. This satirical art really speaks volumes. One is that when life may serve you some fairly large obstacles and barriers, you can still do something. You either use the situation to your advantage or give up and die. The choice is yours.

I remembered once going out to dinner with a buddy of mine. We arrived at the restaurant and were directed to our seats. The restaurant was busy, and the waiters seemed to be running frantically back and forth. After what seemed like an eternity, she finally came to our table to greet us and ask what we would like to drink. We gave our drink orders, and she departed. My friend was obviously upset at the time we had spent waiting; and as soon as she left the table, he referred to her in a racially derogatory way. I was surprised and told him that was not necessary, but he continued with his negative rant. Now a few minutes later, the waiter returned with our drinks and placed them on our table. I went out of my way to thank her as I hoped my buddy would do also but to no avail. She then sighed as if exhausted and managed to put a smile on her face as she asked, "Are you ready to order, or do you need a few more minutes?"

I seized the opportunity and asked, "Wow, its busy today. How are you doing?" I could not make this up folk. It was as if she's just wanting to get someone to ask that very question, and she suddenly broke down while explaining the terrible day she was having, from her home almost being lost to trying to balance her life while working two jobs and raising kids as a single parent. It was obvious she was overwhelmed. I was a little surprise at her venting, but now I had a better understanding of what she was experiencing. I told her to hang in there and that we, my buddy and I, totally understood the matter. Again, she apologized, took our orders, and dashed off to the kitchen.

My buddy's response was a bit humorous as he said, "Wow, didn't know she had all that drama in her life." It seems that small gesture of asking about her day made a difference because her demeanor and attitude, as well as her response to our table, became excellent for the rest of our time there. Before leaving, I made sure to leave a larger-than-normal tip for her. That made me feel good, but I assure you she felt good too. We simply cannot live our lives while hoping that everyone around us simply get it together. It takes both sides doing something. I could have taken the position in that restaurant to push back and demand from her a better attitude and treatment toward us. I could have simply ended the time abruptly without leaving a penny for the tip, but none of these actions would have enhanced her life or mine. In fact, it may have been the single action that may have driven her to the edge. We do have a choice, a responsible choice that is not predicated on other's action but simply on our choice to make a difference to take the high road. Rising above the situation truly gives one a better perspective of the situation. I do not know what became of that waiter, but I feel good knowing that I contributed positively to her life and to the world. Ask yourself: what impact are you making in your environment? Is it a positive or a negative impact?

The unfortunate reality of prejudice is that it is as old as time itself, and as you dig deeper into humanity's past, you are presented with examples of hate, bigotry, and prejudice. In our more recent history, we have large-scale levels of bigotry and innate hate and strife like the genocide of Rwanda during 1994. Here we see rivaling tribe of the Tutsi engaging in a blood slaughter of innocent men, women, and children, mercilessly murdering over eight hundred thousand persons before the international community decided to get involved.

This was not isolated; and as you move from the African continent to Europe, we find another example in the 1990s when Bosnia and Herzegovina declared independence. Here again, we see the Bosnian Serb forces siding with Yugoslavian army to bring slaughter and other atrocities to their Bosnian Muslim and Croatian civilian population. By the end of this manslaughter, over four hundred thousand lives were executed. I can list several more cases of humanity's thirst to draw blood from their fellow human being because of deep-seated hate and mistrust that had festered over time to a breaking point of a dam being released. Many involved in these atrocities even lack the ability to fully understand or articulate the reasoning behind their actions but are simply drawn into the ferocity of those around them as the herd-mentality factor takes over, this demonstration of herd mentality which is really a consolidated and centralized action and focus that no longer requires directions. This is seen in gangs in our own cities as they gun down others simply because of a color or being in a neighborhood not designated as theirs. Other examples are recognized racist groups like the KKK who would not think twice of ambushing and executing minorities or anyone not in support of their way of thinking. The responsible and factual base of all of this is that bigotry and hate exist in all camps. This evil can appear and rear its ugly head in the heart of any vulnerable sole that opens the door and welcomes it in. How many of you welcome this beast into your home, your life, and even your churches? We think we have the ability to control and regulate our own hearts but soon discover that we really do not. Imagine one man, with his superior intelligence and compare him to a lion, choosing to enter an enclosure to face that lion.

Can you imagine any other result other than he will lose and probably be killed? Now if that man plans on subduing and conquering that lion, he must enter that enclosure with some tools like a gun, a teaser, and other restraining devices. Though extreme, this symbolism of the lion and the man is the best I can muster to show the intense forces that are in contention in the arena of prejudice and bigotry. One will win, and so we simply will decide which one of these two forces we are. This is a responsibility each person will have to face regardless of the side they choose.

> Create in me a clean heart, o God, and renew a steadfast spirit within me. (Psalms 51:10)
> Remember, people will judge you by your actions not your intentions. You may have a heart of gold but so does a hard-boiled egg. (Maya Angelou)

Chapter 10

My life journey has really been full of experiences and teachable moments. I will admit that I am who I am as a result of these experiences, learning moments, but, most of all, my total environments' experiences. Our society is so polarized that a large segment of individuals in society have never visited the home of another racial group. Some have never invited another race into their homes or had a meal at a public facility with someone outside of their familiar world, their race. Some reasons are fear, others nervousness, and some simply hate any interaction with other groups be it black, white, Indian, etc. In spite of the reason, one must ask him or herself where this began.

Many blacks still carry the deep-seated resentment, a generational DNA in their hearts that had been passed from generation to generation from the days of slavery. This resentment sees all whites through lens of suspicion; and with that perception, there is a hidden lava of emotion that may erupt suddenly when tapped with the right emotion or the right experience to lash out in defense. For many whites, they too carry a generational DNA with them, one rooted in era of old when their race dominated other groups without restrictions or limitations. Both of these sides exist side by side in our society today as they struggle to assimilate into a world that has transitioned past those more predacious or painful era. It's a wonder we don't see more conflict in our streets.

In spite of this fact of our predisposed makeup, many of us in our own racial group are subjected to or perpetrate on others the same senseless violence and hate we so often love to point at in others. The statistics gathered from the US Department of Justice report "Black Victims of Violent Crime" stated that in 2005, 93 percent of black victims of violence had aggressors that were also black, and 85 percent of white victims had aggressors that were white. When we see stats of this nature, it should be a hard reminder that we are indeed dealing with a heart issue in our society that really transcend race or ethnicity. When we think of the amount of human rights and race relations meetings and conferences that are happening around the globe on any given day, it's interesting that instead of things getting better, they appear to be spiraling to something worse. These meetings and conferences are good; but if nothing addresses the core of the issues which is the heart of man, we're simply applying a Band-Aid to a problem that requires surgery.

Imagine the very next person you meet, whether in the grocery store, the county clerk's office, your coworker, your neighbor, or the man in the street, they may very well be harboring these deep-seated feelings. But guess what, we can't read minds. Since we can't read minds, then we can simply examine our own thoughts, our own feelings, and the stereotypes or prejudices we each carry around. Let our self-assessment yield a positive result, one that is focused on making the world around us better. Martin Luther King Jr. said passionately that "darkness cannot drive out darkness: only light can do that. Hate cannot drive out hate: only love can do that." The thirst to embrace and nurture hate and bigotry is exactly the tool that slowly strangles an individual. I never met a racist or a bigot who appeared to enjoy life. Instead, they were always bitter, suspicious, and in a state of constant turmoil.

I remembered reading an old folklore story of an Eskimo who was out hunting polar bears. His perfect trap was a two-edged knife sharpened to perfection. He buried the handle in the snow with the sharp blade pointing straight up. On the sharp blade, he pours some fresh blood from a young seal. Not long after that, a polar bear approached the knife. Due to its enhanced smelling abilities, he finds what appeared to be fresh blood and starts to lick at the sharp blade. As he indulged, he hardly realized that he was now ferociously lapping up his own blood, a result of the lacerations caused by the sharp blade. This distraction was all it took for the hunter to become the prey and for death to ultimately follow. I believe many in our society are not only experiencing an inability to self-assess, but more importantly, they are experiencing spiritual death. When humanity becomes spiritually dead, he then becomes vulnerable to the uncontrolled abilities of released inhibitions and reasoned emotional responses.

The urge to engage only in the familiar and with only what you know may actually limit your ability to learn, to grow, and to step outside of the boundaries that may define you. We must understand that we are bigger than the immediate threat, larger than the circumstance we encounter, and stronger than that grimacing Goliath we face in life. Remember, engaging in ignorance only enables it. Rather, just flow past it and experience the exhilaration that overtakes you as you realize that spirit of hate, anger, and contempt had no power over you.

I remembered being a shy introvert during my early child hood years. I would force myself to appear confident in public while falling apart inside. One of the most hurtful things I experienced during those vulnerable teenage years was hearing from some individuals, adults at that, say things to my parents like "You have a proud guy there. He doesn't want to play with these kids. He's above them." At times, I would see birthday invitations arriving at the house, and my name would be absent from the invitee list. All of this was because someone simply chose to run on an assumption of who I was. Their assessment was topical in its purest form and lacked substance and foundation. In spite of this insignificant approach to solving problems, many in society embrace this approach to determine their life's journeys. All wasn't lost for me, though. I had great parents who never failed to encourage and motivate me. This support from my parents and those who took the time to cut through the facade and sought to know me found someone real, genuine, and interesting.

Today I find the same approach as one of the most effective methods in relating to persons. It's an approach that ensures persons were a human of integrity first and that it was up to them to prove me wrong. I cannot, for the life of me, understand why some folks can go through life simply being propelled on lies and having no desire to know and be able to embrace the truth. This lie many live with is simply what has become their lives. It's their familiar place, and it keeps them in that box of familiarity. For them to step outside that box of familiarity is to venture into a world of unknown. For many, this unknown world is too fearful and downright scary. Why would they dare venture there?

Many thought Christopher Columbus and his entourage were insane with their petition on venturing across the seas in search of alternate trade route as presented to leaders of Italy, France, England, and Spain. Ultimately through several setbacks and conflict, it was done and new trade routes that were not known now aided in the expansion and beginning of global commerce.

Only those who are willing to step out of their comfort zone and embrace risk, setbacks, obstacles and even ridicule will be able to truly maximize their life's journey. What you think you have now within that box of the familiar is nothing in comparison to the world that awaits you once that box is open; and you allow yourself to fly, venture, to explore, and to learn. We have all seen wealthy men, powerful men, and famous men all succumb to the prison of sticking in the familiar box and were destroyed because they failed to venture outside the box, to learn, to explore, and to understand the rest of the world around them. It is very important to understand that growing knowledge truly empowers; and when that growing and learning stops, you might as well be dead.

Visit a mall or a public event here in the United States. More than likely, you will see persons of all background; but more interestingly, you will run into persons of foreign backgrounds who left their countries and homeland to make the United States of America their home. Most of these individuals, like me, understand that in order to be successful in this nation, they must learn the way of life here. They must learn the language; they have to comply with regulations and standards that are instrumental to our identity as Americans. Failing to adapt to life here in the Unites States will more than likely lead to an unfulfilled life. These individuals become isolated as they attempt to move against the grain of this society. I've had conversations with persons who embrace this radical position and have emphasized to them that they can embrace the new life, the new society and customs though different from theirs. That part of them, their origin will always be there. I can still remember vivid moments in my life growing up in Guyana, times at school with my friends, running along the sea walls, flying kites, and taking trips with my family. These memories will always be a part of me as long as I live even while I'm still being very proud to be an American. My life is richer because of my experiences, and my ability to relate to others who grew up outside the United States gives me the type of dynamic relational association many can only imagine. My life is stronger because of it. Look through the ages of this great country; and you will see that countless persons, like me, came here to make it theirs. Generations later, many have forgotten that part of their history as they spew a message that is hateful and isolationist in its core.

I really do believe that those who are prejudiced lack the component to even love those close to them, and to continue in a perpetual state of bigotry and prejudice is really about getting to a place of being as primates. You see, creatures of the wild may love its infant simply because of instinct but will still kill or harm another infant that is not its own. Humanity's advantage of higher intellect and the ability to empathize and sympathize allows us or should allow us to treat each other with some semblance of dignity, the kind we ourselves would like. When we force ourselves to consciously move beyond this humanistic quality, we then find ourselves moving ever so subtly to the realm of primal adaptive association. This is the type of association that would cause cannibalism where humans eat other humans or someone, the hanging of someone from a tree by the neck because you hate his or her race or ethnicity. This type of primal adaptive association would allow you to rationalize your evil and damning actions and somehow attempts to bring peace to an anguishing soul.

While I worked with some young men in my early years as a mentor, I often experienced many of them becoming angry and more defiant when I confronted them of some realities. Some of these realities were simple messages about dressing appropriately due to the impression given or learning to articulate the English language with competence or being guilty by association in simply being in the company of individuals who were doing wrong. Later when I had conversations with many of these individuals, they would confide in me that the anger they exhibited was really a result of them realizing that what I was saying was true, but they chose to become more defiant in opposing anything I was saying. I believe many in our society are living the same defiance and angry lives as they fight against a message of truth that is loudly telling them their bigoted way of thinking and acting is profiting no one, including them. Though reality may hurt at times, it brings with it a sense of liberation from the chains and bondage associated with living in that ever-toxic box of hate, bigotry, anger, along with the awful disregard of the humanistic approach of life's journey.

I have encountered many individuals over the years who have acted one way, but ultimately it was revealed how different they were from that initial impressions and actions. Be transparent in your perspective and believe. You're helping no one by hiding your bigotry and hate. With transparency, you can then avoid those you would rather not be around and also give those individuals the opportunity to avoid you. The truth allows you, as well as others, to live freely and out of the way of each other.

I remembered reading of a couple and a child who had arrived at a hospital for a critical consultation with a specialist. While waiting in the waiting room, a gentleman came into the room, greeted them, and picked up a magazine and sat down, thumbing through the pages of the magazine. The couple's child just happened to be sitting closer to the gentleman who continued flipping through pages as he glanced at articles. The parents were obviously uncomfortable with this individual being close to their child and decided to relocate the child placing her on the opposite side of them and further away from the gentleman. This move was still not enough and again. They all decided to move down one extra seat to gain some more distance between them and the stranger. A few minutes later, a nurse called for the family to follow her into the offices; and while they waited to be seen, they had no idea that the doctor they were going to be seeing was the same gentleman in the waiting room; he had stepped out for a break. Imagine the look on their faces when he stepped into the room. How often in life do we make these ridiculous errors only to regret our actions later?

> A man that finds friends must show himself friendly; for there is a friend that sticks closer than a brother. (Proverbs 18:24)
> The poorest man in this world is not the man without the money, but the man without people. (African Proverb)

Chapter 11

When we look at the issue of bigotry, hate, prejudices, and racism, we should be observing it through a two-way viewing window. When we view any issue in life, especially pertaining to the matter of discrimination, there should be a simultaneous introspection that is occurring, the kind of inner assessment that digs to uncover any bias first within us. When the conscious assessment is done, it truly allows for a better decision making. I cannot recall the many times that I took the extra time to self assess and because I took the extra time to make this self-assessment, I was able to make a decision that even amazed me after the fact. Many individuals unfortunately do not take the necessary time to self-assess. and that is why we often hear statements as "I wish I could reverse time. I'd do it differently," or the other popular one, "Hindsight is 20/20." How much of life's decision could we better execute if we were to allow ourselves to pause and reflect. This really is an idea that will yield the type of reward in any area of life, from finance to relationships, which we can truly be proud of. Even if you aren't a Christian convert, you can understand the significant of a verse in James chapter 1, "So then, my beloved, let everyone be swift to hear, slow to speak, and slow to anger." This pause prevents haste in our decision making and gives us a better opportunity at living, loving, laughing, and not being in remorse and constant regrets.

I've seen many lives destroy as a direct result of being two persons—the hidden true self and the public persona. As extreme or risky as it may be, it helps one to be honest to themselves first. There is a liberation that occurs with honesty, the type of honesty that is referenced in the scriptures with the statement, "The truth will set you free." This freedom speaks toward more than a physical liberation from jails and the judicial system and attests more to a liberation that resonates from one's soul to bring a peace even in the midst of chaos. It is why we see the numerous examples of individuals who committed crimes actually would have gotten away with it had it not been for their own confession and feeling the need to share this information.

The human experience, good or bad, cannot truly be authenticated unless it is shared with someone. We are not singular in our humanity but very much a compilation of social forces, factors, interactions, and emotions. Those who profess to be islands or isolationist too often result in a degenerative state where rationale and decisions becomes lost in confusion. During this time, they grapple to embrace something in the hope that it will bring that inner peace but to no avail. In the end, they left to their own vices, passions, and belief self-destruct.

Society in general has a way of masking this phenomenon well. The general masses of society can continue moving right along with their individual lives, too consumed to even notice this particular destructive tear in the fabric of our lives and society. If one gets the opportunity to be allowed into this world, they will come face to face with an ideology that is extreme, foreign, and unproductive. They will see that though those who embrace the ideology are living lives that may be falling apart, their addiction to continue embracing it grows with each new day.

In my research of this matter of prejudice and bigotry, an unusual and hard to understand phenomenon is happening. Many of the more poverty-stricken areas of the United States harbor the most hate and prejudice. As I looked deeper into this matter, I began to see a concerning fact.

Many of these individuals direct their frustration and anger of their condition toward other groups. Some direct it toward blacks, others toward whites, and some toward immigrants, all in an attempt to have a clear target for their animosity. It's easier to shoot at a fixed target instead of shooting and swinging blindly in the hope that you will eventually hit something. One of the major discrepancies with this approach is that it completely misuses and overextend their resources, a waste in other words. They fail to see large industrial forces that are directly contributing to their plight from the low pay they receive after working long, sometimes arduous hours in companies and factories but having nothing to show for it. They fail to see a taxation system that appears to punish the hardworking individual while delivering to the wealthy loopholes and shortcuts to keep more and more of their already-laden pockets. This fight is generally fed through streams of tradition and stereotype. With that, you can expect to hear claims as it's the blacks or Hispanics causing this, or it's the white man trying to keep us down. The narrative runs freely, void of fact and substance in many instances, but it facilitates that inner thirst and hunger to hit a target, someone, somewhere, and whomever.

It is important to note that prejudice and bigotry will never cease in our lifetime. It is an unfortunate but innate nature that resides within each of us. Its potential to be released and shared has to be balanced constantly and daily as we go through life. If we are unwilling to venture outside of our personal sphere, we will live unaware of life outside of it. It doesn't mean the outside world does not exist but only that you have chosen either consciously or unconsciously to not become familiar with it.

It reminds me of a business presentation I attended. The individual was applying for a professional position in the institution I was working in, and his presentation was part of the process. During his presentation, he referenced living and working in a larger city with a more social and racial homogeneity and how isolated he felt. In fact, he compared his experience to pretty much wearing a camouflage outfit. I thought this was rather revealing, and that interesting reflection I had at that moment was probably only in my head alone. To give you some perspective, everyone in the room listening to the presentation was white except for me and one other person. I don't think others reflected on his statement about wearing a camouflage outfit. This may have been seen or heard by them as him simply being in a weird place; therefore, the simple answer was getting out of it and finding another place. What I heard reflected something different and familiar. This is an experience I have experienced so many times and in so many settings I cannot remember all of them. I can remember how it made me feel. His description summed it up in that small statement.

When we are in a relaxed or comfortable environment, it is easy to simply dismiss anything else as insignificant or not applicable to the moment, but this still does not remove the reality of the matter. To this argument, I will introduce the well-known question: when a tree falls in a forest and no one is around to hear it, does it make a sound? It simply becomes a philosophical discussion versus a discussion on empirical truth. When it's all said and done, that tree still fell either from a weakened state, a lightning strike, or any other existential force that may have contributed to its fall. Your presence or mine at the time of the incident does nothing to change the fact of the matter, a tree did fall. It is why this subject matter will continue to be one that brings passion, discussions, and emotions to the surface of one's life. These issues are anchored deep inside each of us as we move through our lives, and left unchecked, they simply erupt, leaving regrets, devastation, and remorse along the way.

It is true many unintentionally isolate others in society without thinking about it. It's just an automatic compulsion we all share that navigates us toward the familiar and steers us past and away from the unfamiliar. Instead of your focus being on our humanity, many attempt to appease the circumstance by focusing on our nationality or other physical distinctions.

I remembered as a young airman in the United States Air Force, I hung around with some cool guys who happened to be white. We really were like brothers in arms. I had arrived at my base located in Colorado, and one of the briefings we received was about protecting yourself from the sun when outside. This was very important, but because of the high altitude, we were more susceptible to the sun's rays. One weekend, I went swimming with friends at an outdoor pool in the area, and after a long day on that summer day with the sun at its peak, I didn't notice how terrible I had been sunburned. The next day, I woke up to my skin having a burning and itching sensation, and not long after, I began to have layers of my skin just peeled off. When a few of my buddies noticed this, they almost sang in unison, "Wow, I didn't know black people get sunburn."

That day, I simply used it as a teachable moment as I responded jokingly to them, "Man, you guys have a lot to learn." Together we laughed, but I have always remembered their sincerity in that proclamation. They were not hateful to me. In fact, they were some of my best friends during those early Air Force years but just innocently ignorant of what the facts were as it pertained to the dark-skinned individual and the sun's exposure. How many times we allow innocent ignorance to impede our ability to build meaningful relationships. What is needed is our ability to rise above the initial flood of emotions that generally are the first to surface. If we are not vigilant enough, we will miss countless opportunities to build our circle of relationships and increase our sphere of the familiar. I am truly blessed to have friends of all race that are dear to my heart.

This does not mean I as well as my different race of friends didn't have to contend with surfacing prejudices, stereotypes, and learned conditioning gained over our lives. We all made the decision to dig deeper, break down, and step over the familiar boundary and explore life beyond our self-imposed boundaries.

> With man this is impossible, but with God all things are possible. (Matthew 19:26)
> No matter what accomplishments you make, somebody helped you. (Althea Gibson)

Chapter 12

The Bible paints a wonderful picture of those who stand the test of time through suffering and persecution. Our victories aren't achieved because we go through life unscathed by trials of life but quite the opposite. I know of wealthy and seemingly successful persons who committed suicide in a final attempt of finding peace. Folks, peace can only be achieved in our inward man first when we begin to see life through the eyes of Christ. Romans chapter 5 verse 3 in the Bible reads, "Not only so, but we also glory in our sufferings, because we know that our suffering produces perseverance, character, and character, hope. And hope does not put us to shame." When we look around in society, we will discover many who face tremendous adversity and defeat but stood resilient and on the promises of faith in God to rise again and be victorious.

Don't fall victim to your negative experiences. Learn from them but don't let them consume and corrupt you. For one to hate the one who murdered a loved one is for you to become a murderer yourself. Remember, hate promotes and cultivate more hate, but only love and forgiveness suffocates and strangle those negative forces around us. One of my favorite Bible passages is Proverbs chapter 25, verses 21 and 23, which says, "If your enemy is hungry, give him food to eat; if he is thirsty, give him water to drink. In doing this, you will heap burning coals on his head, and the Lord will reward you." This is not talking about a literal fire of coal on their heads but instead is addressing how we can suffocate hate for that ultimate victory over those who hate.

The well-known words that were once uttered by Rodney King following his encounter with Los Angeles police, "Why can't we all just get along?" sounds simple, logical, and easy to do when we simply look at life through unrealistic lens. This is so because life itself is about good and evil, high and low, cold and hot, right and wrong, and many more. So true it is of this balance of life that biblical scholars wrote in the book of Ecclesiastes chapter 3, verse 1, "There is a time for everything and a season for every activity under the heavens." He went on to explain this as he painted a picture we all understand with death and life, joy and pain, tears and laughter. It was so from the beginning of time and remains so today; we will always have hate, love, peace, war, and more clashes between spectrums and opinions.

My passion has been and will continue to be one that focuses on significantly minimizing those elements that are counterproductive to our very existence. It is hate and bigotry, a systemic deluge that poisons and destroys humanity. Until we decide to embrace truth, it will continue to evade us all, hiding in clear view. I can say this without reservation about the friends, associates, and strangers I know over the years who have dealt with serious anger issues. They have fallen into the clutches of either hate, prejudice, unforgiveness, or the deadly and profound case of self-hate. Change in our lives, society, situation, and personal areas must begin with a focus on hope. I challenge you to let that hope begin with Jesus Christ and to accompany it with a determination that you can and will see change. That change may be small or large but begin with you.

Many in our world have the success story written about their lives. Most of the world simply sees the aftermath when success and triumph became visible. The journey that is often filled with obstacles and tough times are often unheard and unseen. These individuals didn't allow the tough times to consume them but instead allowed it to fuel them along their journey.

We read of significant figures in our history like Abraham Lincoln who suffered an unusual amount of setback in his life. From failing in a business venture, being defeated when he attempted to run for a US senate seat and losing a nomination for Vice President of the US. All of these setbacks and more didn't stop him from one day becoming President of the US. Reading his story reminds me of the bible verse in Philippians 4:13 which says "I can do all things through Christ who strengthens me".

Hope is a powerful human attribute that can only be achieved through a deliberate and persistent practice of our responses to life's itself. It isn't an automatic response but instead must be cultivated.

Hope is so powerful to human existence that it can save lives and guide one through devastating circumstances. The biblical equivalence to this thought is proverbs chapter 13 and verse 12 "Hope deferred makes the heart sick, but a longing fulfilled is a tree of life".

Do not allow hate, stereotypes, opinion of others, or your experiences to determine your potential and your destiny. Let today's rejection open doors of opportunities, and in so doing, we can suffocate the forces that are constantly seeking to kill, steal, and destroy our lives and hope. I am so grateful that through God's love and compassion, I have established solid friendships over my life. These friends are indeed a melting pot of different races, nationalities, and personalities all playing a vital part in who I am today. Folk, you cannot imagine the distance you will go when you remove the personal barriers and those social and deep-seated biases. The old African proverbs says, "If you want to go fast, go alone. But if you want to go far, go with others."

Many struggle with this ideology, even Christians. A familiar passage of scripture in the Bible makes reference to Christ eating and drinking with sinners. Christ later corrected his followers who questioned him about his association and passionately shared an example that doctors don't work on persons that are healthy but are primarily there to attend to those that are ill. We cannot desire change in the world and in our society unless we are willing to be a part of the change we desire. You desire more love, then love more. You desire more peace, then be more of a peacemaker. You desire more friends, then be friendly. This simple but profound process of sowing and reaping applies to grace, mercy, forgiveness, compassion, and favor. Christ wired humanity this way, and it will guide us on a path to success when we follow it.

PRAYER OF SALVATION

Making the decision to serve Jesus Christ begins with this simple but profound prayer;

> "Lord Jesus, forgive me of my sins. Wash me clean with your precious blood. Fill me with your Holy Spirit and give me the strength to live everyday for you. Lord create in me a clean heart and renew a right spirit within me, in Jesus' name amen!"

Now that you've made the awesome decision to live for Christ, I want to encourage you to get a bible and begin reading from the book of Matthew. I encourage you to find a bible believing church where you can grow together with others in the faith.

About the Author

Paul Ross, a native of Guyana, South America, has a reputation for being pragmatic in his assessment on life. As husband and father of four, he prides himself in being painfully honest, first to himself and then to others around him. This book dives into some of the more private and taboo aspects of human relationship with particular sensitivity in exploring prejudice, bigotry, and hate.

His first book, *The Killer from Within: Politics in the Faith*, started a dialogue in the Christian community that both provoked and motivated individuals across the Christian spectrum. He has served as an administrative pastor, a college administrator, an adjunct faculty member teaching business principle, and a teacher of biblical principles. He earned a bachelor's degree in technical management and a master's in management in project management.

CPSIA information can be obtained
at www.ICGtesting.com
Printed in the USA
LVHW022355210621
690829LV00006B/265